Greater Works 2.0
A Compilation of Prayers for Everyday Life

Visionary Author: Sonja Pinckney Rhodes

Contributing Authors:
Rev. Patricia W. Crawford
Dana P. Richardson
Sherri Pinckney Kinloch

Greater Works 2.0

A Compilation of Prayers
For Everyday Life

Some of the scriptures in this book were taken from the King James
Version - Bible in Public Domain; New International Version (NIV)
Holy Bible, New International Version®, NIV® Copyright ©1973,
1978, 1984, 2011 by Biblica, Inc.® Used by permission; The ESV® Bible
(The Holy Bible, English Standard Version®). ESV® Text Edition:
2016. Copyright © 2001 by Crossway, a publishing ministry of Good
News Publishers. Used by permission; and NEW AMERICAN
STANDARD BIBLE®, Copyright © (NASB)
1960,1962,1963,1968,1971,1972,1973,1975,1977,1995 by The Lockman
Foundation. Used by permission.

For information on the content of this book, email
GreaterWorksPartners2@gmail.com

JMPinckney Publishing, LLC
Goose Creek, SC 29445

Printed in the United States of America
ISBN 978-1-7377290-1-3

Table of Contents

Acknowledgements

Many thanks to all whose work, research, prayers and support assisted in the completion of Greater Works 2.0, second edition; especially to Sonja Pinckney Rhodes, Rev. Patricia Crawford, Sherri Pinckney Kinloch and Dana Price Richardson for continuing in the legacy of blessing others through the written word of prayer.

Special thanks to those who gave their time to read, pray for and with us, for your unfailing love extended toward us that poured into us as our spiritual insight was refined through this creative and anointed process.

We are eternally grateful to our families, friends, Pastor, and loved ones near and far for your contributions, encouragement and dedication through and by faith. We are appreciative for Mary Pinckney, Jon M. Pinckney, Sr., Markita Pinckney, Andre' Rhodes, Pastor Byron L. Benton, Derrick Kinloch, Frank Crawford, Cameron Richardson, Ashlen Richardson, Sam J. Price, II, Renee A. Price, Deslin M. Price, and Avia P. Smith, Lillie M. Fields, Barbara A. Calvary, Marcus Gathers, Marlin Burwell, Evelyn Burwell, Thaddeus Doughty, Leon Wrighten, Eddie Fields, Gertrude, the late Yolanda Burwell Jefferson, Rev. Dr. Samuel J. Price, Sr. and Rebecca F. Price

Thank you for your patience, faith, understanding, love, prayers, cooperation, endorsement and for celebrating with us always.

We dedicate these prayers to all those who feel lost, lonely, forgotten or overwhelmed.

Most of all, we give God all the Glory for choosing us to be His ambassadors to bless others that is in need of prayer, restoration, healing and deliverance.

May the Almighty God richly bless all of you

Introduction

Greater Works second edition is an awesome testimony of four valiant women of God from different backgrounds, experiences, and walks of life who accepted their call to share how God is continuing to transform their lives. They have penned so graciously their witness of His mighty works. Through prayers that speak volumes of their journey, you will experience how God held, carried, covered, sustained, renewed, and restored them, within each page. You'll feel their strength and growth into the character of God. The personal witnessing of His goodness and His grace is resounding for others to be inspired, delivered, and set free by His marvelous and miraculous works.

The unspoken determination impelled these women of God, Sonja Pinckney Rhodes, Rev. Patricia Crawford, Sherri Pinckney Kinloch and Dana P. Richardson to be willing vessels, outpouring as of living streams of flowing waters, conveyed through the thunderous waves of dreams dared to dream, hurts they overcame, despairs turned into hope, and triumphant victories. They all attest to the pivotal aspects of their lives that once spiraled through rising currents that were strengthened through their persistent prayers, by trusting God to bring them through their journeys of how He brought them over, through and out. Their prayers testify to the great work God continues to do in their lives, as stated in John 14:12, *Verily, verily, I say unto you, He that believeth on me, the works that I do shall he do also; and greater works than these shall he do; because I go unto my Father.*

Ms. Sonja Pinckney Rhodes
Visionary Author

Psalm 1:2-3(KJV)

2 But his delight is in the law of the LORD; and in his law doth he meditate day and night. 3 And he shall be like a tree planted by the rivers of water, that bringeth forth his fruit in his season; his leaf also shall not wither; and whatsoever he doeth shall prosper.

Ms. Sonja Pinckney Rhodes is the Number One Bestselling Author of From Pain to Purpose: *A Bridge Over Troubled Waters*, published in 2019, the visionary author of Greater Works: A Compilation of Prayers for Everyday Life, the owner of JMPinckney Publishing Company, a South Carolina Realtor for Carolina Elite Realty, a retiree of nearly 30 years of service for the State of South Carolina and a volunteer advocate for My Sister's House for battered and abused women.

In addition, Ms. Rhodes is the advisor for the Young Adult Ministry, advisor for the Baptist Young Women Ministry, and she teaches biblical principles for the Young Adults, ages 18 - 36 years old at Mt. Moriah Missionary Baptist Church. Sonja is a Minister of the gospel, an e-Life Facilitator, and a team leader for the Charleston Area Justice Ministry (CAJM).

Ms. Rhodes earned her Master's Degree in Business Management with a Minor in Human Resource Management at Strayer University in 2014.

Ms. Rhodes is also the recipient of the 2021 South Carolina House Resolution Award, the second highest lifetime achievement awarded to a South Carolina resident, by the Honorable South Carolina State House Representative Wendell G. Gillard. She will be listed in the State Book of Records for life.

Ms. Rhodes is a native of Charleston, South Carolina; the proud mother of two sons, Jon Michael Pinckney, Sr. and Andre' Christopher Rhodes, mother-in-law of one admired daughter-in-law, Markita Flemons Pinckney and three beautiful grandchildren, Jon Michael Pinckney, Jr., Ari Samiya Pinckney, and Nia Malika Pinckney.

Inspiration

As I accepted the call as a prayer warrior for an international prayer line that holds an average of 1000 listeners for 15 minute segments, in my despair, I cried out to the Lord to fill me, speak in me, and to speak out of me, that I may know the needs of those listening for an answer; and He did. His Word says, "to call unto me, and I will answer thee" (Jeremiah 33:3).

The Lord began to awaken me in the middle of the night with prayers flowing out of me like rivers of living waters. I launched prayers with my phone's flashlight illuminating just enough to write at 3 a.m. and 4 a.m. for the prayer line to be a blessing, to touch a heart, to heal a wounded spirit, and to save someone from detrimental thoughts and actions. It was never me, but the Lord. I shared my experience with my Pastor, Dr. Byron L. Benton, and he answered, "If the Lord tells you to write, then you write. You don't know who need those prayers or what woman can't pray for herself."

I sought the Lord deeper, and He birthed this awesome mission in my spirit that would bridge others to experience His glorious prayers of affirmation, confirmation, healing, and deliverance.

Prologue

Dear God, My Lord, Savior and in Whom I Trust:

Thank you for the rising of the sun and the going down of the same. You are worthy to be praised. We thank you Lord for life, for health and for strength and for the dawning of a brand new day. Lord, I thank you for food on my table and clothes on my back. Lord, we couldn't make it to another day without Your grace and Your mercy. So, God, we thank you for being Jehovah Jireh, our provider. You promised never to leave us alone even when we don't understand and especially when our backs are against the wall. The Prophet, Isaiah, tells us that when the enemy comes in like a flood, You will lift up a standard against him. So,

> We're standing on Your promises, Christ our King, that we cannot fall, listening to the Spirit's call, resting in You, Savior, our all in all, as we stand on Your promises God.

> Your Word is a lamp unto our feet and a light unto our path; therefore, we lean not to our own understanding but trust You in all thy ways that you may direct our paths.

Oh God, You said not to fear men in their faces because You have not given us the spirit of fear but of love, power and of a sound mind; even in the midst of CoVid-19, You are still God. You are our refuge and strength; A very present help in trouble. You wrap Your loving arms around us and keep us safe from all harm and danger. Even when we don't understand the social and racial injustices, You remind us to lean not to our own understanding and to trust You in all thy ways that You may direct our paths. As we come to You, we are reminded to look to the hills whence comes our help, because our help comes from You; our maker and creator, our beginning and our end; our Alpha and Omega. You have all power in Your hands and from the very beginning, You were God. You are God alone and You are from everlasting to everlasting. There's no God above You, none that stands with you and none will come after You. You are the only living and true God, the Sovereign Lord and majesty of the universe. We understand that You are loving, as well as Holy and righteous, merciful and gracious, as well as just. We know that You will forgive our sins and judge them, as well. Only because of You we can face tomorrow, because of You all fear is gone. We know You hold the future and life is worth living just because You live. Oh God,

> our hope is built on nothing less than Jesus'
> blood and righteousness. We dare not trust
> the sweetest frame, but wholly lean on Jesus'
> name. Oh Christ the solid rock we stand, all
> other ground is sinking sand.

Lord, God, as we put our trust in You, we can do all things because You strengthen us. As we put our trust in You, all fear is gone. As we put my trust in You, we are more than conquerors. As we put our trust in You, we can walk by faith and not by sight. Oh God, if we put our trust in You, we can say to the mountain, be thou removed and it shall be done. You, God, have given us authority to trample over the serpent's head. You have sent us forth as sheep in the midst of wolves, and told us to be ye therefore; wise as serpents and harmless as a dove.

Wisdom comes from You, God, and as we humble ourselves, pray and seek Your face, turn from our wicked ways, then You will hear from heaven and will heal our land. Let us, brothers and sisters, seek ye first the Kingdom of God and His righteousness, that all these things will be added to us, because we can do all things through Christ who strengthens us. We are the head and not the tail; and our comings and goings are blessed; and we are confident that the good work You have started, You will finish. So, we press on to the mark of the high calling in Christ Jesus. Not looking back in regret. Not holding on to the old man. Not reminiscing, but casting all our cares upon You because You care for us. Because You are the way, the truth and the life; You will lead us in the paths of righteousness. As we stand on Your promises, we cannot fail.

We thank You that You know the plans You have for our lives; that is to prosper us and not to harm us and to be in health and to give us a hope and a future. Even though the enemy walks around like a roaring lion seeking whom he may devour, we have confidence in You, Lord, that we are protected in Psalm 91, that covers us under Your wings of protection; 1000 may fall at your side and 10,000 at your right hand but it shall not come nigh to us. Because You are the author and finisher of our faith, You will keep us in perfect peace whose mind is stayed on You. We thank You for sending Your angels to watch over us. All night and all day, Your angels are watching over me my Lord, All night - all day, angels are watching over us.

The Power of God's Unfailing Love

Lord, we thank You for Your unwavering and unfailing love that formed us into Your image. We honor You and adore You, for You are worthy of all our praises. Because of Your love, we have life more abundantly. It was Your love that was beaten and bruised for our transgressions. It was Your love that endured the cross. It was Your love that bled and died for the sins of the whole world. It was Your love that laid down that we may have hope. It was Your love that got up with all power in Your hands that we may partake of the bread of life. The bread that feeds our souls and makes us whole. The bread the sustains and the strengthens us. The bread that heals us from all of our souls diseases. The bread that keeps us safe from all harm. The bread that washes our sins away. I know the bread to be the lifter of my head and the lover of my soul. It's nothing but Your love that can reach from the highest mountain to the lowest valley by and through the blood that was shed because of Your enduring love. Lord, we love You because You first loved us. Without Your love, we would be lost like a ship without a sail. Without Your love, we would not be forgiven. Without Your love, life wouldn't be worth living. And without Your love, we wouldn't know how to love.

We thank You for Your L.O.V.E.
Life Outstretched Offered & Victoriously Exalted

In the name of Jesus, I offer my heartfelt love. Amen

Expressions of Love

_____
_____
_____
_____
_____
_____
_____
_____
_____
_____
_____
_____
_____
_____
_____
_____
_____
_____
_____
_____
_____
_____
_____
_____
_____
_____
_____
_____
_____
_____
_____

Amazing Grace

(a song of praise)

By Celtic Woman

Amazing Grace, how sweet the sound
That saved a wretch like me
I once was lost, but now am found
Was blind but now I see

Was Grace that taught my heart to fear
And Grace, my fears relieved
How precious did that Grace appear
The hour I first believed

Through many dangers, toils and snares
We have already come
T'was Grace that brought us safe thus far
And Grace will lead us home

Amazing Grace, how sweet the sound
That saved a wretch like me
I once was lost but now am found
Was blind but now I see

Lord, we thank You for Your Amazing Grace that reminds us that we are forgiven and redeemed by the blood of the Lamb. Although our sins may be as scarlet, they shall be white as snow; though they be red like crimson, they shall be as wool. What a promise to behold from You, our Savior, who died on the cross for our sins and rose with all power in Your hands that we may receive the fullness of Your grace that redeems our wretchedness, removes scales from our eyes, and reconciles us to You through and only by Your blood that was shed on the cross… that we may also extend the hand of grace to others, as You have demonstrated towards us. We thank You, God, for Your grace through Jesus, our Christ. Amen

God's Amazing Grace

Adoration

Oh Lord, how excellent is thy name in all the earth. Angels bow before You; Heaven and earth adore You. What a mighty God we serve! And as I look back over my life, I can see how you have guided me, how you have protected me and how you have kept me. You have been so good to me and You keep on blessing me. Yes, every time I turn around, You just keep on blessing me! And when I think about the goodness of Jesus and all You have done for me, my soul cries out HALLELUJAH! Thank You, God for saving me! Amen

God, You're Amazing

_____
_____
_____
_____
_____
_____
_____
_____
_____
_____
_____
_____
_____
_____
_____
_____
_____

Savior, Savior

Our Lord and Savior,

We thank You for thinking of and loving us so much that You gave Your only begotten Son to save sinners like us; the One who was blameless, but answered and obeyed the quintessential call as a ransom to pay the debt of the whole world. Who also, endured the walked of shame; was wounded for our transgressions, bruised for our iniquities: the chastisement of our peace was upon Him; and with His stripes, we are all healed… it was of no crime of His own, but that of ours that we might not perish, but have everlasting life. Unto Him we owe our all.

By the power of His shed blood on that old rugged cross, we have eternal life. Because the blood never loses its power; it reaches the highest mountain and the lowest valley; it cleanses our sin-sick souls and gives us strength from day to day. We thank You, God, for washing us in the blood of Jesus. Although our sins are as scarlet, they are now washed white as snow, all because of the blood of Jesus.

And when we call on His great name, demons have to flee, scales are removed from our eyes and shackles are broken, just like the woman with the issue of blood. We just need to touch the hem of our master's garment to be made whole. We need a touch from You, Lord, as we press our way for healing of our souls; as we press our way for healing of our minds; as we press our way for healing for our bodies, our families and our jobs. Everything we need, God's got it in the palm of His mighty hands, but we must have the faith of a mustard seed to know that He's already worked it out.

We may be troubled on every side, yet not distressed, we are perplexed, but not in despair; persecuted but not forsaken, cast down, but not destroyed.

Let us remember before the beginning, You were there. Before we were even thought of, You predestined our lives, ordained and sanctified us. Therefore, no weapon that is formed against us shall prosper and every tongue that rises against us in judgment shall be condemned. So, God, as we stand on Your promises, let us not be conformed to this world but be ye transformed by the renewing of our minds to prove that which is that good, acceptable, and perfect will of God.

As we close this prayer, by the mercies of God, we present our bodies as a living sacrifice, holy, acceptable unto You, God, which is our reasonable service. Now to the only wise God our Saviour, be glory, majesty, dominion and power, both now and ever. Amen

Go in peace and go make disciples for Christ

Savior, Savior

I Will Walk By Faith, Even When I Can't See Because God:

Is My Refuge and Strength	Psalm 46:1
Will Strengthen Me	Isaiah 40:31
Knows that Plans for My Life	Jeremiah 29:11
Works All Things for My Good	Romans 8:28
Is My Provider	Matthew 7: 7-11
Cares for Me	I Peter 5:7
Will Not Forsake Me	Deuteronomy 31:8
Will Act	Psalms 37:5
Will Direct My Path	Proverbs 3:5-6
Cannot Lie	Hebrews 6:18
Always Listens	I John 5:14
Is a Peacemaker	Isaiah 26:3
Is a Teacher	Psalm 32:8
Makes our Way Straight	Isaiah 45:2
Is Our Strength	2 Corinthians 12:9-10
Is a Peacemaker	Philippians 4:6-9
Will Fight for You	Exodus 14:14
Is Our Protector	Psalm 91:3
Is Our Shield	Psalm 28:7
Is Our Help	Psalm 121: 2
Is Our Savior	Roman 10:9-10
Supplies all our Needs	Philippians 4:19
Is a Giver of Good Gifts	Matthew 7:9-11
Our Keeper	Isaiah 54:17
Anoints Us	Isaiah 61:1
Friend	Proverbs 18:24
Lifter of our Heads	Psalm 3:3
Inhabits our Praise	Psalm 22:3
Died for Us	I Peter 2:24

Faith

Wisdom

My son, pay attention to what I say; turn your ear to my words. Do not let them out of your sight, keep them within your heart; for they are life to those who find them and health to one's whole body.
Proverbs 4:20-22

You see, God gives us His wisdom through His Word. He speaks to us in all things. We must make it intentional to listen for His small still voice. It will keep us from harm, it will keep us safe from those who judge unjustly, and it will lead us into fellowship with Him. For He knows the thoughts He thinks toward us; those are thoughts of peace and not of evil, and to give us an expected end. There is hope, and He is our refuge. Know that we are covered under the blood that never loses its power.

Father God, in the name of Jesus, we come before You as humble as we know how, honoring you, blessing you and worshipping You, as we enter Your gates with thanksgiving and into Your courts with praise. Father God, we lift our hands to thee and bless Your name. There is no other help we know; for You are worthy of all our prayers. We glorify You for Your name alone is excellent.

We come before you, Father God, with praise on our lips. Father, we come to you, oh God, with prayer in our hearts. We come to you, God, because we may be broken or lost. Oh God, we come to you because, Lord, we know that you are the way, the truth, and the life. Lord, we just come before You because we know You said to come to Jesus and to come to Him right now; to come to Jesus while we have time (Rev. Charles Nicks).

We know not the hour, nor the day, we don't know which direction to go, we don't know what to pray for or how to pray, in fact, we don't know anything unless we seek Ye first the kingdom of God and Your righteousness. We don't know Father God, unless You hold our hands, Lord. We don't know unless You speak to our hearts and we hear Your small still voice. We seek You, and lean on You, and depend on You for we know that You are the author and finisher of our faith and we can't do anything without you, Lord.

We come to You because You brought us out of darkness, Father, and into Your marvelous light. We come to You Father God, because You are our teacher and our guide, so we seek You, and we cast our cares upon You. Your Word says You would never leave us nor forsake us.

We come to You, Lord, because above You, there's no other. We commit our minds to You, we submit our thoughts to You, we give You our plans, and turn our lives over to You because You are our Shepherd, and yea though we may walk through the valley of the shadow of death, we will fear no evil because You are with us. Therefore, we put our complete trust in You, Lord. Thank you, for you alone are the true and living God and everything belongs to You. In Jesus' name, Amen!

Wisdom

God is our Everything

Most Eternal and Everlasting Father,

We thank you for being the light of our salvation, our beginning and our end, for the dew of freshness every morning, and the gift of a new day. We thank You for being our Lord, our God and our Savior. You alone are our Rock in a weary land and our shelter in a time of storm. We realize that if it had not been for You on our side, we don't know where we would be; for you are the reason that we are able to live, move, and have our being. It is the very essence of You that called our names and we were able to rise to see another day. And as we look back over our lives, we can see how you have guided us, how You have kept us and how You have never left us. We stand on Your promises that will not fail, knowing that no weapon that is formed against us shall prosper. Even in the midst of these trying times of social injustices, racial profiling, racism, gun violence and an invisible virus that walks about seeking whom it may devour, we will continue to hold on to Your unchanging hands and trust You in all our ways to direct our paths.

We believe Your word to be true in knowing that when the enemy comes in like flood, You will lift up a standard to block every plot and plan. Therefore, we must put on the full armor of God to protect us from its fiery darts. But we know that You will keep us in perfect peace whose mind is stayed on You because we trust in You. But Lord, when it seems like all hope is gone, Proverbs gently reminds us to lean not to our own understanding and to trust You in all our ways that You will direct our paths. For we know not the way but we know that You are the way, the truth and the life and Your word says that You are our strength and shield, an ever present help in trouble.

You will not suffer thy foot to be moved and He that keeps thee will not slumber. So, we have peace knowing that You will keep us in all our ways and that nothing can pluck us out of the Master's hands.

Thank You God for Your reassuring Love, Grace and Mercy. In Jesus' name. Amen

God Is Everything

Peace

Dear God,

Without peace, we cannot comprehend all that You have for us; how You made the Universe and all that exists within. How Your thoughts are higher than our thoughts. How You lined up the stars, moon, sun, and planets that they may have its own purpose; to light the darkness with stars that shines so brightly, the moon to illuminate the sky in the same place for everyone to see; how the sun warms the earth, brightens and rises for a dawning of a new day; and how the planets are orbited and stands where You have commanded.

Lord, we know that You orchestrated our lives in order the same way. You have predestined us and called us out of darkness into Your marvelous light. You've made us to be liken stars, the light of the world when we walk with you in obedience. As the songstress, Odetta, so sweetly sang, "this little light of mine, I'm gonna let it shine. Everywhere I go, I'm gonna let it shine." (Harry Dixon Loes). We know that when we tap into You, You give us the light others may see. Therefore, God, we lift You up knowing that You will do the drawing of all men unto You. As we draw nigh to You, You will draw nigh to us. Thank you, Jesus, for making our crooked places straight and perfecting all things concerning us. Thank You for turning our lives around and placing our feet on solid ground; You put running in our feet, clapping in our hands and joy in our hearts. And if we stand still, God will put a song in your spirit and turn your tears into joy because, the joy of the Lord is your strength.

Brothers and sisters, stand still and see the salvation of the Lord. You may be going through a test, but He'll give you a testimony, we may not understand the trial and tribulations but remember His Words says in Proverbs to "lean not to our understanding, to trust Him in all our ways and He will make our paths straight." We must give all our worries and concerns to God, who is the author and finisher of our faith. He knows all about our troubles, and if we go to Him, He will make our sorrows bright; He'll make a way out of no way. He'll turn our midnight into day, because weeping may endure for a night, but joy comes in the morning.

Continue to trust in the Lord, and He will set you free. Whom the Lord has set free, is free indeed. God can do all things but fail because He is the great I am. He is our all in all. He can move mountains just for you because you are the apple of His eyes. He thinks the world of you.

Begin to thank God in advance for the plans He has for your life knowing He will prosper you and give you hope and a future. Heavenly Father, we honor, praise, and worship You for paying the price for us while we were yet still sinners. In Jesus' name we seal this prayer. Amen.

Peace

Talk with Jesus

It's okay to have a little talk with Jesus as the songstress says, I once was lost in sin, but Jesus took me in. And then a little light from heaven filled my soul. He bathed my heart in love and wrote my name above. You will find that a little talk with Jesus makes things right (Cleavant Derricks).

Father God in the name of Jesus, we come before you to give you thanks on this day that You have made. While rejoicing, we give thanks to You for your grace and for your mercy. Thank you for waking us up in our right minds today. Thank you for life, for health, and for strength. Thank you, Lord, that we have movement in our bodies and our minds are healthy and clear.

Thank you, God, for a place to lay our heads and that our lying down last night was not in vain or that we didn't awaken at the judgment-seat this morning. Thank You, Lord, that we were able to get up and move about and have food on our tables to eat. Thank you for providing all our needs, according to Your riches in Glory, God.

Thank You, Lord, for taking us to and fro, and for blessing us with jobs but Lord, we know that You alone are our provider and our jobs are just our seed. Then, Lord, You kept us all day long from dangers scene and dangers unseen, from chaos, and exposed mistakes. You even kept us from the arrow that flies by day and the destruction that wastes at noonday. Then you brought us back home, and we found that everything was in its proper place. There was no breaking in or no going out. And even though Lord, there are storms on the ocean that moves our way, we know that our souls are anchored in Jesus and we will not drift away (Bishop Ronald E. Brown).

Lord, we know that You calm the seas and You quiet the storms in our lives just by Your spoken Word that says, peace be still. Even the winds and the waves obey You. We thank you, oh God because You're so good to us. And we thank you, Lord, for all those who have gone before us; our parents and ancestors who introduced us to You and struggled for righteousness and stood on the foundation of Your Word that was laid for us. Lord, we are nothing without You.

Help us to think on those things that are true, noble, right, pure, lovely, and admirable in all things, as we honor you. In the name of Jesus, this is Your servant's prayer. Amen.

Talk with Jesus

Our Rock

Dear Father God in Jesus' Name! Thank you once again for the opportunity to come before You and for life, health and strength. Lord, we know we can't do anything without You. Without You, we would fail. When we feel inadequate, when we feel we're not enough, and when we feel our voices don't matter, remind us that we are more than conquerors through Christ Jesus who loves us, that we can do all things through Christ who strengthens us, that no weapon that is formed against us shall prosper.

Lead us to the Rock of our salvation. The Rock that will keep us from falling, the Rock that will never fail, the Rock that will never leave us nor forsake us; for when we are weak, You are strong. That Rock is Jesus, the Alpha and Omega of our being; the beginning and the end; our wheel in the middle of the wheel and because of You, we can face tomorrow.

We can't do anything without You, oh God. Therefore, we put our complete trust in You, who is the author and finisher of our faith. Without You, we are nothing; without You, our lives have no meaning. As we step out in faith, we trust You, God, who knows all about us and hears our faintest cry. You know our comings and our goings; our beginnings and our endings. You know our thoughts before we think them and You are able to do all things but fail. You are our heart regulator, and a mind fixer. You pick us up and turn us around then place our feet on solid ground. We are never in too deep where He can't reach us. He will reach way down to pick us up because; God specializes in healing and restoration. If you go to Him, He will set you free, if you go to Him, He will make you see because where there is no hope, He will give you hope and where there's sadness, He'll give you joy (Tri State Mass Choir).

There's nothing too hard for Him. He is the great I am. He can do all things but fail. Try Him and see. He will put clapping in your hands, stumping in your feet, and He will show you great and mighty things. He will stir up the gift inside because God is able to make all grace abound to you.

So, lean not to your own understanding. Trust God in all your ways, and He will direct your paths. He wants the best for you, and He wants you to win, regardless of your situation or what you've done. He wants to heal you and set you free from bondage. The enemy wants you to stay in the box; the box of denial, the box of fear, the box of defeat, the box of sickness. But God has come to set you free from the lies of the enemy. Humble yourselves, pray, seek His face, and turn from your wicked ways, and He will heal you from the inside out.

You'll look at your hands, and they will be new. You'll look at your feet, and they will be new, too. Your walk will change. Your talk will change, your company will change, and your thoughts will change. Resist the devil, and he will flee. Trust the process because God will never leave you alone and if He calls you to it, do it because He has already equipped you for the journey. Your life was predestined before you were in your mother's womb, so don't dismiss those thoughts of greatness. It's not the darkness that frightens you; it's your light. God has created you to do great things, and as you step out in faith, you liberate others to do the same.

Go where God sends you, do what God has called you to do because you can do all things through Christ who strengthens you. God, we thank you that all things work together for the good of those who love you and who are the called according to Your purpose. In Jesus' name! Amen.

Jesus is our Rock

Refuge

Have not I commanded thee? Be strong and of a good courage; be not afraid, neither be thou dismayed: for the Lord, thy God is with thee withersoever thou goest.
Joshua 1:9

Our strength comes from God. Our success comes from God, as well. We can't earn it, and we can't work for it. It's all controlled by God. We must obey God even when we can't see what the results will be and when we are not certain what to do or how to do it. Set aside time each day to read and meditate on God's Word, and then remind yourself of God's Words day and night. Act today on what you know God has said, and God will strengthen you and assure your success in carrying out his purpose for your life.

Father God, in the name of Jesus, as we seek You today, we thank You for Your Word found in Psalm 46 that says, "You are our refuge and strength, a very present help in trouble". Therefore, we will not fear. We will be still and know that You are God. We will not, Oh God, walk in fear over our finance, our family, our future, our health, or our faith. We will, Oh God, be still and know that what You have promised, will indeed come to pass for us. We thank You, oh God, for the covering of Psalm 46, that helps us to not walk by sight when we see roadblocks, dead ends, closed doors or negative outcomes, but to walk by a faith that says, if God be for us, who then can be against us. Lord, we thank you for giving us ears to hear what you have to say. We seek the divine testimonies of Your Word, and Your divine order that we may be in good health and have complete healing. Know that you are due for physical healing in your body, spiritual healing in your soul, and an emotional breakthrough in your mind. Jeremiah 30 says, "God will restore health unto thee, and He will heal thee of thy wounds".

We know that all things are possible to all that believes, and we are healed by all 39 stripes that Jesus bore on the cross at Calvary. And it's at the name of Jesus, that every knee shall bow, and every tongue shall confess that He is Lord.

Today, Lord, as we face trials and tribulations, Psalm 46 reminds us that You are our refuge. You are our strength, a very present help in trouble. Therefore, we will not fear, though the earth be removed, and though the mountains be carried into the midst of the sea; Though the waters thereof roar and be troubled, though the mountains shake with the swelling thereof. We will be still, and know that You are God and will be exalted among the heathen. So, Lord, we ask for strength to wait on You and to be of good courage that You will strengthen our hearts. This is my humble prayer, oh God. In Jesus' Christ's name, know that it can and will be done. Amen!

Refuge

All Have Fallen Short

*Even the righteousness of God which is by faith of Jesus Christ unto
all and upon all them that believe: for there is no difference: for all
have sinned and come short of the glory of God; being justified freely
by His grace through the redemption that is in Christ Jesus.*
Romans 3:22-24

Father God, in the mighty name of our Lord and Savior Jesus
Christ, we humbly submit ourselves to You knowing that you
are the author and finisher of our faith; knowing that we can't do
anything without You; and knowing that it's only because of
Your grace and mercy that we are saved.

We come to You because You are the God of our salvation,
above You, there is no other, and You are God and God alone.
We know that you created us, You created the heavens and the
earth and everything that dwells in it belongs to You.

Lord, You cause the sun to rise and the sun to set, because
You are Sovereign. You bless those whom You wish and harden
the hearts of those whom You choose. Lord, I thank You for
choosing me. You predestined our lives and made a way out of
no way. Thank You for making the crooked places straight and
perfecting all things concerning us. You have already made a
way of escape, and You have blocked the enemy in his tracks,
even when the enemy is within us. God, when you show Yourself
to us, and we are still disobedient, You still provide, You still give
us new mercies every day, and You still forgive us for our
shortcomings. The book of Romans reminds us that we all sin
and fall short of Your glory. Lord, because of Your grace and the
price You paid on the Cross, we are declared righteous.

Purge us, Lord, that we may be clean. Wash us so we may be whiter than snow. Make us hear joy and gladness; that our bones which have been broken may rejoice. I thank you, Lord, that you thought we were worth saving. So, You came and changed our lives. You thought we were worth keeping, so You cleaned us up inside. You thought we were to die for, so You sacrificed Your life so we could be free, and whole and tell everyone we know (Anthony Brown & group therAPy).

Lord, we praise You, we worship You, we glorify You, because You deserve it. It is You who hold our today and tomorrow in the palm of Your hands. The Lord *will give grace and glory: no good thing will he withhold from them that walk uprightly.*

So, Lord, we thank You for everything. My brother, my sister, what sin are you playing with? What thoughts are you contemplating? Are you attempting to ignore the voice of the Lord? Repent and turn from sin. Offer your life to God. Today is your day to repent! For all the wrong you have done; for the times you strayed away, Repent! For judging others; and for the times we doubted the Lord, just repent!

Our lives were created with a purpose; never allow sin to destroy it. Establish your faith in the Lord. I am convinced that nothing can separate us from the love of God. In Jesus' name, Amen.

Thank You for Your Grace

_____
_____
_____
_____
_____
_____
_____
_____
_____
_____
_____
_____
_____
_____

Provider

Father God, I thank you for life, health, and strength. Thank you for making ways out of no way. Thank you for delivering us from Egypt even when we didn't want to let go. Thank you for the manna you provide and freshwater that fills us every day.

Your Word says, You will never leave us nor forsake us (Hebrews 13:5). If you feed the birds and they don't worry about food, You will supply our every need because, You are Jehovah Jireh, our Provider. You are more than enough for me (Brooklyn Tabernacle Choir).

Your truth is our shield and buckler. Knowing that gives us the confidence to go on and see what the end will be. If we give up, the enemy wins, but we are more than conquerors in Christ Jesus; our comings and goings are blessed, and no weapon that is formed against us shall prosper.

So, God, we put our trust in You because our hope is built on nothing less than Jesus' blood and righteousness, we dare not trust the sweetest frame but wholly lean on Jesus' name (Edward Mote). We thank You, God, in all things and for all the many ways you have made for us. In Jesus' name, Amen.

You are my Provider

Stand

Dear Heavenly Father, in the perfect name of Jesus. We come before You today to give You praise, for not only showing us the way we should go but for being the way, the truth, and the life. God, thank you for the assurance of Your safety, privilege, power, and Your mercy. We realize that the dwelling place of God lies within us.

We thank you for your mercy and for your grace that covers us every day. We thank you that Your fountain is ever flowing to cleanse us from our sins. Lord, if we listen to Your still small voice, You will lead and guide us into all truth.

We know that You will open doors that were once closed in our faces. Places that denied us will begin to approve us because You are our way-maker and light in the darkness. We will follow You, God, and stand on Your promises. *When you call on God, believe that He is a rewarder of them that diligently seek Him.* So, stand and if all else fails, continue to stand still until you see the salvation of the Lord.

God, we know that our *thoughts are not Your thoughts, neither are Your ways our ways.* We will continue to stand on Your word. What has God spoken into your life? What has the Lord appointed you to do? Who are you waiting on? Only wait on God. When you have done all you can, and you have waited long enough, step out in faith. Take with you *the whole armor of God that ye may be able to withstand in the evil day, and having done all, to stand. In Jesus' name. Amen*

Stand Still

Purpose

Dear God in Jesus' name. Thank you for another opportunity to call on Your name as our Lord, our Savior, and our God. Although we may take it for granted and it seems to be a cliché, Your names are the very essence of our being. God you have given us a purpose to create, recreate, succeed, overcome and tell how we got over. You have given us purpose in our mental state, emotional state, physical state, and spiritually. Your Word says when we are weak, you are strong; therefore, we stand on Nehemiah 8:10 that says "the joy of the Lord is our strength".

As we walk by faith and not by sight, as we seek Ye first the Kingdom of God and Your righteousness, as we call upon You, forsaking ourselves and lean on Your understanding that Your word may be a lamp unto our feet and a light unto our paths. We thank You for peace that surpasses all understanding that will guard our hearts and minds in Christ Jesus; and for the spiritual confidence of knowing who we are and whose we are… the very purpose You have for us.

God, we ask that you cover us, keep us, strengthens us, and bless us to walk away from those things, situations, and people that hinders our growth and from fulfilling our purpose in You. Thank you, God, that You have not given us the spirit of fear but of love, power, and of a sound mind. Because of You, we can do all things through Christ who strengthens us, and our comings and goings are blessed.

Thank you that our pain has purpose and Your plan is what's best for us. Lord, it may not feel good, and others may talk about us, walk away from us and treat us differently, but we thank you for sanctifying us for Your purpose.

Thank You for making our enemies our footstool, seating us at the table before our enemies, and anointing our heads with oil in the presence of our enemies. In Jeremiah, we read that You know the plans You have for our lives; to prosper and not harm us and to be in health. We know that You are omnipresent, omnipotent, omniscient, and You are more than enough.

We thank You for carrying us in our times of sorrow and loneliness, I thank you for forgiving us in our disobedience. We thank You for keeping us when we were too lost to keep ourselves. God, we thank you for protecting us from the enemy and when we go astray; we thank You for Your saving grace. We give You the honor, the glory, and all the praise. For we can't do anything without You. In Jesus' name, we pray. Amen.

I Have Purpose

Thanks

Father God in Jesus' name, we thank You for the opportunity to be in Your presence, to bow before You in prayer, to thank You for another day. What a blessed miracle to be here among the living; another chance and another opportunity to be ambassadors for You. I pray that You order our steps, and I pray that our hearts and minds hear and receive Your direction for today; that we are leaning and depending on You to walk in our purpose.

Only You, Lord, can make our crooked places straight; only You Lord can open new doors and pour out blessings that we don't have room enough to receive. And, God, when You close doors, let us not grow weary in well-doing; remind us through Your Word that weeping may endure for a night, but joy comes in the morning.

We know that a closed door is not always a "no". A closed door may be to wait on You, and to be of good courage that You may strengthen our hearts and minds. Victory is already done. Peace is already made. Deliverance is already finished. We call those things that are not as though they are. The new job is on the way. That new house is on the way. That disobedient child is on the way. That bad marriage is mended, sickness and diseases are healed. Depression is turned to joy. Anger is set free. Loneliness is liberated, and no weapon formed against you will prosper.

We thank you God that You have already predestined our lives to walk in Your favor; to be above and not beneath; and to be more than conquerors through Christ Jesus. We thank You for life, health and strength. We thank You for Your amazing grace and undeserving mercy. Without Your grace, we would have been consumed.

Thank you, God, for another chance and for new beginnings. You've been better to us than we've been to ourselves. You saw fit to call our names, so we thank You for choosing us from the belly of our mother's womb. You already knew our names and our destiny. Sometimes we forget our names, but like the prodigal son, You welcome us back into Your royal family, where the feast of the Lord is going on.

Thank You, God, for never leaving us alone or forsaking us. Thank You for looking beyond our faults and seeing our needs. Thank You for looking at our hearts, as men look on the outside. Help us to lean not to our own understanding but to trust You in all thy ways that You may direct our paths. God, we know that you reign on the just as well as the unjust and You have no respecter of persons. Help us to be Your hands and feet to be a blessing to others. Comfort hurting hearts and spirits. Strengthen us, as You are the lifter of our heads. Thank you for being our solid rock that never fails.

Thank You for Your grace and mercy. Lord, we thank You in all things and through all things. We can't do anything without You. Thank You, God, in Jesus' name, Amen.

I Give You Thanks

Strength

Do not sweep my soul away with sinners
Psalms 26:9

Lord, we know that you did not give us the spirit of fear. Just as David feared for his life and prayed from anxiety because of his past sin, we also wonder if all our sins will be pardoned or remembered. Because of our weaknesses, lack of faith, little courage, compromised love, and the many temptations, it brings on a fear that we may not enter the realm of the saved. We may find ourselves praying to God, please don't sweep our souls away with sinners or unbelievers. But be not dismayed, whatever betide, know that God will take care of you and He will not sweep His children away with sinners. Continue to walk with outward integrity and inwardly trusting in the Lord?

Dear God, our Father, we thank you for ripping the veil that we can approach the altar with humble hope and hearts as *we seek Ye first the Kingdom of God and Your righteousness, that all things may be added unto us.* Lord, please give us patience to not give up and the strength to stand strong in Your Word as those who have gone before us.

Lord, you have told us not to fear. But Lord, although we trust You, we also fear that we may die without hitting the mark of the high calling, while settling for mediocrity, or fear of settling for less than Your best for our lives. Help us to resist the devil that he may flee and that he may not talk us out of what You have in store for us. We know the devil comes to kill, steal, and to destroy or bring trouble, confusion, and chaos. But, God, You can deliver us out of the hands of the enemy every time. The bible says to resist the devil, and he will flee. Teach us to trust

You, God, for the strength to endure difficulties and the faith to wait for You.

Help us not to be conformed to this world but transformed by the renewing of our minds; knowing that God is able to make all grace abound toward us, having all sufficiency in all things. It's only by Your grace, God, that the joy of the Lord is our strength. Although things may change, and we feel all alone, and our hearts are broken, the *Lord's hand is not shortened, that it cannot save; neither His ear heavy that it cannot hear.*

Lord, help us to defeat the lies of the devil with Your truth. Help us to live boldly and believe that we are *fearfully and wonderfully made* and to be *confident that He who has begun a good work in us will complete it until the day of Jesus Christ.* These blessings we entrust in Jesus' name, Amen.

Strength

God be Glory

If any man speak, let him speak as the oracles of God; if any man minister, let him do it as of the ability which God gives: that God in all things may be glorified through Jesus Christ, to whom be praise and dominion forever and ever.
1 Peter 4:11

How is God glorified when we use our abilities? He is glorified when we use them as He directs us to help others. Only then, they will see Jesus and praise Him for help they have received. Peter said to let your light so shine before men, that they may see your good works and glorify your Father which is in heaven. God is able.

Father God, in the name of Jesus. Oh Lord, we come to You boldly, we come to You hastily, we come to You confidently, and we come with expectancy because we know without a doubt that You are Lord and that You are God. We heard Your voice that said *come unto me, come all who labor and are weary, and I will give you rest. For My yoke is easy, and my burden is light.*

We know that You are God and You're able to do just what You said You would do. We know that You will fulfill every promise to us. We know that You are able to do exceeding and abundantly above all that we can ask or imagine. You are Lord over our lives. We know, Lord, that *You have not given us the spirit of fear but of love, power and of a sound mind.* We are encouraged in knowing that You will bless us, give us breakthrough, favor, opportunities, opened doors, and supernatural healing that will erase years of frustration that ruled in our lives.

God, Your Word says that *Your blessings will chase us down and take us over.* So, Heavenly Father, we pray to grow spiritually and be more like You. We choose to trust You in times of adversity knowing that You are working things out for our good.

Lord, please renew a right attitude within us so we may walk uprightly in Your Kingdom and be true ambassadors for You. For we know that there is much work and we pray that you equip us with courage, boldness, strength, and the love of Christ to *call those things that are not into existence.*

Lord, we also know that *our timing is not Your timing, our thoughts are not Your thoughts and our ways are not Your ways.* It may be late in the midnight hour that you decide to turn it around, but we know that it's gonna work in our favor (Fred Hammond)! Isaiah says to, *wait upon the Lord, and He will renew our strength.*

We thank You, God, for turning things around and knowing that we can *run and not be weary.* The Lord says, *touch not my anointed and do my prophet no harm. He is a rewarder of them that diligently seek Him.* Then you can sing, God has smiled on me. He has set me free. God has smiled on me. He has been good to me (Rev. James Cleveland). Amazing Grace, how sweet the sound that saved a wretch like me. I once was lost, but now I'm found. Was blind but now I see (Chris Tomlin).

Brothers and sisters, know that God is able to *lead you beside the still waters.* He will make you *lie down in green pastures.* He will *restore your soul.* He will *lead you in the paths of righteousness for His name's sake.* He knows your purpose, and you will go further with God if you put Him first and make your spiritual life a priority. He would *never leave you nor forsake you,* so we can boldly say, *The Lord is our Helper, we will not fear what man can do unto us.* In Jesus' name, we pray, Amen

God Be Glory

At the Altar

Dear Heavenly Father, we come in Your name at this very hour, this very moment to give Your name the praise, the honor, and the glory. Knowing that this is where You hear and answer all our prayers. It's at the altar where we press our way. It's at the altar where we reach for the hem of Your garment. It's at the altar that we lay our burdens down. It's at the altar that You hear our faintest cry.

Lord, we thank You for the altar experience that we can walk away, look back and see where You have brought us from, and how You have turned things around. Lord, Your grace and Your mercy watches over us all night and all day, and we thank you God for Your Son, Jesus, who died on the cross for the sins of the whole world. That's because You have all power in Your hands, it's because *Your name is above every name and You can do all things except fail*. Knowing this we have the very confidence in You that we can do all things in You and through You. Because of You, Lord, we give You glory, honor and praise.

Thank you for this opportunity of prayer because we know that You hear, and you answer prayer. We know that prayer is the key that opens the door. We know that prayer changes things. We know that prayer confirms our trust and our belief in You. Thank You, that through prayer, we have the blessed assurance that we belong to You, God.

Friends, God knows what He is doing. He has it all planned out—plans to take care of you, not abandon you, plans to give you a future and a hope (Jeremiah 29:11). Leave your prayers at the altar, and God will take care of you. In Jesus' name, Amen.

At the Altar

God is the Great I Am

I am He – the Messiah

I am the bread of life

I am the Living bread

I am the light of the world

I am the door

I am come that they might have life

I am the way, the truth and the life

I am the resurrection and the life

I am in the Father and He in me

I am the true vine

I am the Good Shepherd

I am that I am

His name shall be called Wonderful, Counselor, Mighty God, Everlasting Father, Prince of Peace (Isaiah 9:6)

Over-comer

_____
_____
_____
_____
_____
_____
_____
_____
_____
_____

Prayers of Positive Confessions

I am more than a conqueror	Romans 8:37
I am successful	Joshua 1:8
I am prosperous, strong & courageous	Joshua 18-9
I am a new creature in Christ	2 Corinthians 5:17
I am redeemed	Galatians 3:13
I am delivered	Colossians 1:13
I am the righteousness of God	2 Corinthians 5:21
I am saved	Romans 10:13
I am sanctified	I Thessalonians 5:23
I am healed	I Peter 2:24
I am the head and not the tail	Deuteronomy 28
I am worthy	Ephesians 4:1
I am predestined	Ephesians 1:5
I am an heir of God	Romans 8:17

I can do all things through Christ who strengthens me
Philippians 4:13

Who Does God Say You Are?

Rev. Patricia W. Crawford

Revelation 22:2 (KJV)
"In the midst of the street of it, and on either side of the river, was there the tree of life, which bare twelve manner of fruits, and yielded her fruit every month: and the leaves of the tree were for the healing of the nations."

Rev. Patricia W. Crawford is an Associate Minister at Mt. Moriah Missionary Baptist Church. Dedicated to serving God and His people and passionate about prayer and teaching; her ministries include Grief and Recovery, serving as the spiritual teacher for the Women's Auxiliary, and coordinator for the Upper Room Prayer ministry. She also serves as Chaplain for the Women's Clergy of the Charleston County Baptist Association. She obtained a Bachelor of Science degree in Commerce from

North Carolina Central University and her Master of Public Administration from the College of Charleston and the University of South Carolina. Rev. Crawford is married to Frank Crawford, Jr. and they are the parents of two daughters, Allison C. Ford (Cody) and Kristen M. Crawford and they are the grandparents of two adorable grandsons Daniel, and Ethan Ford.

Faith

Our Father and our God, You've spoken in your word that whatever we ask for in prayer and in your name, if we believe that we have received, it will be ours. Thank You for re-affirming and building our faith to trust in You and Your word. We ask Lord that You will increase our faith from the measure that we have all been given to greater faith. Build us up in the most holy faith with the power for us to believe that through You all things are possible. Since our faith walk requires us to live by believing and not seeing, we ask that You will strengthen us in our weak areas. Your Word says that faith is the substance of things hoped for and the evidence of things not seen. We know that without faith we cannot and will not be able to please you. With faith nothing shall be impossible for us.

We ask You, dear God, to help us in every weak area of our faith walk. Give us overcoming faith to believe and know that what You have spoken over our lives shall be accomplished for Your word does not return void, but accomplishes what You send it to do. Holy Spirit, we ask that You will be our divine teacher on new lessons of faith. Show us what faith looks like, how to exercise our faith in hard times and difficult days. Lord we need increased faith in times and seasons of distress and discouragement. Help us on the days when life makes no sense and we look at the state of the nation and the world and we see that many have fallen in a state of doing what is right in his own sight. Give us the kind of faith that will help us to always trust You and never lean unto our own understanding. Our ways cause us to err, stumble and fall when we lose sight of your direction and guidance. Help us to help ourselves by continuing to study Your word and to hear Your word so that our faith can grow stronger day by day. Thank Your Father for hearing our prayer and help us to ever be mindful of the need to stay at Your feet and in Your presence. Draw near to us as we continue to draw near to You.

Matthew 11:16, Hebrews 11:1, Luke 1:37, Romans 10:17

Faith

Inspiration

The urgency to participate in this writing project results from a divine inspiration from God Himself. When you are confronted with a "God wink" moment and when God gives you a personal invitation to join Him in His work; there is no alternative but to realize, as Paul says in Philippians, that "it is God who is working in you, enabling you both to will and act for His good purpose." It is not a coincidence that participating with the church in the 42 day reading of the "Purpose Driven Life" that God presented this writing opportunity that compels me to complete the writing of the last three chapters of the book that He has been waiting for me to finish. My involvement with this project confronted me with a direct command from God to finish the work! In so doing, my purpose intersects with destiny so that His will for my life is fulfilled through blessing the lives of His people.

The opportunity to write a series of prayers with Sonja Pinckney Rhodes and these wonderfully chosen and ordained women of God is an answer to prayer for my own struggles to finish the work that He assigned. Not knowing how or what to do, I prayed, and He has provided people, talent, resources, and the help needed to complete the assignment.

As He has answered my prayers time and time again, I believe that as you read these scripture based prayers that you will be inspired and reassured that God is a faithful and prayer answering God. He has solidified my call to a lifestyle of prayer and the call to minister with dedicated prayer warriors who have been called by God to the Upper Room Prayer Ministry at Mt. Moriah. I'm grateful to an awesome God who has shown me favor, along with these women, to write for His honor and glory. Surely, He has rewarded me for faithfulness to the prayer ministry as a warrior and an intercessor. May these prayers bless your life, inspire and encourage you as you make prayer a lifestyle and daily commitment to pray without ceasing. To God be all the glory!

Inspiration

Prayer of Praise and Worship

Oh Lord, how excellent is Your name in all the earth! You are great and greatly to be praised! Our souls do magnify and lift You up. Marvelous are Your works and that our souls know very well. The earth and all therein declare Your glory, and we bring You the sacrifice of praise. Our lips shall praise the Lord, our hearts rejoice, and our souls magnify You, Lord, for You are the great and awesome God. Truly, Lord, there is none like You in all the heavens or the earth. You are the great God, and the earth declares Your glory. Lord, You are Holy and righteous in all Your ways, and we thank You for bestowing Your blessings upon us. Through You Lord and through Your being and Your doings we know that You are God and God alone. Thank You for allowing us the privilege of drawing strength and power from You. Great is Your faithfulness unto us, and we give You thanks for the daily impartation of new mercies in our lives. Our spirits rejoice in You as we bow down in humbleness of heart to worship You in spirit and in truth.

Give us the grace, Dear Lord, to render unto You our best praise and our best worship with the excellence that You deserve. We acknowledge Your excellency and Your majesty Lord and all the days of our lives we shall lift Your name in praise and adoration. For all the good things and for all the wonderful blessings that You have bestowed upon us, we shall never forget Your works. With our whole hearts, we shall glorify Your name and honor You all the days of our lives. Our hearts rejoice in You Lord from the rising of the sun to the going down of the same for Your name is to be praised. Our souls love You, Lord, for you are the glorious redeemer and our righteous judge. Thank You for being our everlasting, and eternal God for You have rescued our lives from destruction and put praise and thanksgiving in our hearts and lives forever.

In the name of Jesus, we pray and seal this prayer. Amen.

Praise and Worship

Trust

Our Lord and our God, we come in the strong and powerful name of Jesus, first to bless Your name, then to tell You how much we love and adore You. We come into Your presence to cast our cares upon You. While they seem overwhelming in times of crisis and difficulty, we know that nothing that we face is greater than You or Your ability to handle it. As the Psalmist writes in Psalm 37:5, *we will commit our way to You Lord and trust You to act on our behalf.* The challenges in the world affecting our lives and livelihood are challenging our faith. Our lives are under attack from the forces of darkness that threaten us and attempt to destroy us. We see lives being lost and no immediate end to worldwide crises, yet we trust You in the midst of the storms of our lives.

We trust You, dear God, for all that we stand in the need of for You have promised to supply all of our needs according to Your riches in glory. We trust You Lord even when we can't trace You, even when it seems You do not hear us, even when it seems that the answers to our prayers will never come. We trust You Lord for we know that You keep Your promises and Your word will not return void, but will accomplish what You send it to do. We trust You for health and healing, we trust You for salvation and deliverance. We trust You in the midst of hardship and difficulty, trials and tribulations, and circumstances and situations. You promised to never leave us nor forsake us even in the midst of all that comes against us. Behold You are always with us, even to the end of the world. We trust You and thank You for the ability and capacity to trust when all else fails us. Your Word assures us that we can trust You because You have told us to not fear because You care for us and You are always with us. You promised to never leave us nor forsake us.

So Lord, help us not to be anxious for anything, but to trust You for everything. Help us to trust in You with all of our hearts and never lean on our own understanding, but to acknowledge You in all of our ways. Your wisdom and knowledge is far greater than ours. Remind us that we can trust You because You are our strength and shield. You are the great God in whom we trust to be our strength and shield. We trust You to guide us through darkness and dangers seen and unseen. We will stand still and know that You are the great God of our salvation who keeps covenant. Our hearts trust in You as You command us to be strong and courageous. Thank You for the fruits of trust that manifest themselves in our lives. We ask for answered prayer and blessings in the name of Jesus. Amen and Amen.

Proverbs 3:5, Psalms 28:7, Joshua 1:9

Trust

Prayer for Salvation

Our Lord and our God, You are not slack concerning Your promises and are not willing that any should perish, but that all should come to repentance. When the enemy snaked his way into our lives, You planned the way for our salvation, redemption, and deliverance. We thank you, Father, that from the beginning of time Your plan for our way of escape from eternal damnation was through the death of Your only begotten Son, Jesus Christ. Thank You personally for my way out of sin, darkness, and death into Your marvelous way of salvation and eternal life. Thank You, God, for loving us so much that You desired none should be lost and that we should all come to You with the inquiry "what must I do to be saved?"

Lord, we give You thanks for putting a hunger and desire in us to want to know You as Lord and Savior. Open our hearts continuously to be thankful for the gift of eternal life. Help us Lord to be bold in sharing the way of salvation with others who do not know You. Empower us to share the good news of the gospel of Jesus Christ so that others will believe and be saved. Lord let there be no fear and apprehension in telling others how we confessed with our mouths and believed in our hearts that You raised Your Son Jesus from the dead. Help us to share with those who don't have a relationship with You that the only requirement is to make that confession of belief to receive You as Lord and Savior.

Hide Your Word in our hearts so that we have an answer for everyone that needs to know that the way of salvation comes from being made right with You, Father. Thank you, Lord, for justifying, sanctifying us, and making us new in You. Help us, Lord, once we have been saved and delivered from our sins to walk in the liberty wherein we have been made free. When we stumble and fall, remind us that we have an advocate through Jesus who will restore us into right relationship with You Father. Lord, let us forever be mindful that Jesus made the ultimate sacrifice through His death on the cross so that we could avoid eternal death and live unto righteousness. Lord for these and all blessings from You, we give You thanks, praise, honor, and glory in the name of Jesus. Amen

Acts 16, Romans 10, Galatians 5

Salvation

Good Success

Lord God, Holy and majestic is Your name. We call upon Your name, for You, Lord God are worthy to be praised. With our whole hearts, we will praise Your name for You are a great and awesome God! We will bless You at all times and praise Your Holy and righteous name. You alone are the great God who exercises kindness, justice, and righteousness in the earth. We give You thanks for being the triune God whose tender love and mercies are new every morning. Father, we thank You for being a faithful and dependable God who never ceases to amaze us. You are gracious to make our ways prosperous and to give us good success as we allow Your Word to feed us and nourish us spiritually.

Father, we ask that You help us to continue to grow in knowledge of Your Word and Your truths so that we can handle the affairs of our lives wisely. Help us with our desire to be faithful and obedient in all things concerning our lives. Lord give us the ability and desire to spend more time in Your presence and in Your Word so that we might learn of Your plans and Your purposes. Father help us to align ourselves with your plans and purposes for they are not meant to harm us, but to allow us to prosper for a hope and a future. Lord, we ask that You continue to allow favor and blessings to rain down on us.

Lord, we thank You, and we praise You for guarding us from fear and worry as we pursue Your will for our lives. Give us the mind of Christ so that we might operate with a mind of clarity, excellency, and accuracy. Remind us that the promises of the Lord are yes and amen and that what You have spoken and ordained for our lives shall come to pass. Your favor surrounds us at all times and in all places as we represent You in the

Kingdom. You have made us stable and secure in our occupations and in our ministries.

Thank You, Lord, for giving us the ability to excel in our performance and to succeed in our assignments. You give us power and might; You give us confidence and assurance, and so we trust You Lord with the fulfillment of our destinies. Lord it is You that protects our hearts, our minds, our character, our esteem, and our reputations so that we remain successful in our ability to accomplish our missions on the earth. Father, our minds rest in knowing that You are in control of all of the details of our lives and every aspect of our existence. We rely on You for continued success and we give You thanks for answered prayers. Amen

Jeremiah 29, II Corinthians 1

Success

Hope

Our Lord and our God, we give You thanks for Your thoughts of peace and not evil toward us. We are grateful, dear God, that in You we have a future and a hope. When we hope in You, our hope of glory, we find strength for weary souls, strength for every challenge, and peace in the midst of confusion. We find consolation in You as we trust You and trust Your word. Your hope fills us with joy, with peace, with satisfaction and a blessed assurance that all is well because of You. Father, our hope is built on Your word and Your promises.

We hold fast to our hope and we do not waver because we know that He who has promised is faithful. You are a faithful God that we can depend on for all things at all times. You strengthen our hearts and cause our hope to increase and we thank You for giving us courage in the midst of uncertain times. Father Your hope causes us to be strengthened in You and Your power. Your hope reminds us that we are never alone for You keep us in all Your ways. We hope in You, Lord, because You are our portion, You are our protector; You are our priest and provider. Father we have a living hope because Your Son Jesus was resurrected from the dead and in You we find the hope of Your glory as we endure hardness as good soldiers. Thank You for the privilege to hope in You and Your Word. Amen and Amen

Colossians 1:27, I Peter1:3, Romans 5:5, Psalms 130:5
Hebrews 10:23, Jeremiah 29:11, Psalms 42:11

Hope

Direction

Father God, we come once again with praise and thanksgiving to seek You for direction. Thank You for giving us a roadmap in Your Word that admonishes us to trust in You with our whole hearts and to lean not unto our own understanding. We are blessed in knowing that if we acknowledge You in all our ways, You will most assuredly direct our paths. Your Word is a light unto our paths and a lamp unto our feet that shows us the way in darkness. You are our helper and our guide, and we need never worry when You lead us in the paths of righteousness. When our ways seem dark and dreary, You are the source of light that brings us to a place of safety. We realize Lord that except You guide us and direct our paths, we will be lost and drifting in a place of hopelessness and despair. You are the source of all that we need in life.

Thank You, Lord, for the times that we don't have answers for the problems and circumstances that confront us, but yet You come to our rescue. We ask that You continue to walk with us in times of fear, frustration, anxiety, and distress. Walk with us in times of confusion and discord. Be our guide, Lord in times of uncertainty and doubt. Let Psalm 91 and the name of our God Jehovah-Nissi be the banner of direction over our lives. Give the angelic host charge to hover over us and to accompany us on this journey of life. Continuously keep us hidden under the shadow of Your wings, keep us close to Your bosom and keep us hidden until the calamities of life pass. Give us continued wisdom and revelation for direction in the critical times of need in our lives.

Lord, we acknowledge that it is You and You alone who orders our steps and establishes us in Your ways so that our feet do not stray. We are Your sheep, and You are our shepherd, lead us Lord in the way that we ought to go. Let Your rod and Your staff continue to guide us. Father, we ask that You continue to comfort us. Lord, let our hearts continue to delight in You so that we never wander aimlessly in life. Keep us from drifting and floating through life as desert tumbleweeds so that we never accomplish the purposes that You have ordained.

Thank You for being the God who makes our darkness light and our crooked ways straight. Let Your will be done in our lives. Remind us time and time again that You Lord are our very present help who rescues us when we lose our direction. Thank You for being our advocate and our intercessor who gives us words of comfort as You assure us that You are with us always and will never leave us nor forsake us. We trust You, Lord, to continue to show us the way and to continually lead us in the paths of righteousness. Thank You for Your blessed assurance and for Your spirit that leads us into all truth. We bless You and praise Your name forever and ever. Amen.

Direction

Strength To Endure

Father, we thank You for the assurance that You are our God; our present and our current help. You assure us in Your word that Your joy is our strength. Thank You for reminding us that You will strengthen and help us. Therefore, we should not be dismayed or distressed. Your strong right arm gives us strength. You are our strength and our song and we are ever so grateful. Lord, in these times of stress, turmoil, trepidation and fear of life threatening diseases; in the midst of challenges that we have never faced before; we come boldly to Your throne to ask for help and strength to endure these turbulent, perilous, and troubling times. In the midst of hurricanes, earthquakes, fires, floods, wars and rumors of wars, pestilence in the land, and the love of many waxing cold, it is comforting to know that You are our source of strength for the journey and trials of life. Lord, we are thankful that as we face grief, distress, isolation, mental anguish and turmoil, you remind us of Your sufficiency and the power of Your Word.

Thank You for reminding us in the book of Nehemiah that we don't have to be entrapped in grief and sadness for the *"joy of the Lord is our strength"*. You have reminded us not to be fearful or dismayed, for You give us strength to endure and to hold on to Your unchanging hand. You alone are our God and we thank You Father for the blessed assurance of being our God and that You have the power to do all things. Strengthen us to endure hardness as good battle warriors and help us to stay on the prayer wall. Lord, we ask that You will continue to be our strength and our shield, our refuge and strong tower as You help us to hold on and endure as we wait for our change to come. In the hard times, the lonely times, the disappointing and discouraging times, we ask Father, that You will strengthen and empower us to believe You. Help us anticipate and expect that You will be the source of power needed to endure the hard times, the difficult days, and the tough hours, days, weeks, months and years. Thank You Lord for hearing and answering our prayers, for truly You are our only source for strength to endure, as You help us not to grow weary in well doing and to keep the faith. Amen and Amen

Galatians 6:9, Nehemiah 8:10

Strength to Endure

Meet the Needs

Great, eternal, and everlasting God our Father, the one who has promised to be a very present help in the time of our needs, we enter into Your presence to give You thanks and adoration. Thank You for being a prayer answering God, who knows what we need even before we ask. Your Word instructs us to ask so that we will receive. Your Word informs us that we have not because we ask not. Lord, we are so grateful that You supply all of our needs according to Your riches in glory. Father, we are thankful that the earth is Yours and the fullness thereof. You own the cattle on a thousand hills, and every good and perfect gift comes from You. Thank You, Lord, that we can access the wealth that has been laid up for us as heirs and joint-heirs of our Father's riches. Continue to be the supplier of every good and perfect gift that we long for.

Father, we are thankful that You have given us good gifts and great blessings beyond our ability to fathom or to even comprehend. You, Lord, are the great Jehovah Jireh, the provider of all our needs. As El Shaddai, You are the all-sufficient one whose help is adequate for fulfilling our desires and wants. As Elohim, You have the ability to create all things in every manner that is needed. When we lack faith Lord, increase our ability to believe and to trust You to honor Your Word so that it will do what You have commanded. Increase or faith to believe that You will do all that You have spoken, declared, and decreed over our lives.

When we are impatient and its looks as if You are not answering our prayers and meeting our needs, help us to be patient and wait on Your timing for the delivery of all that You have promised. We are thankful Lord that You have spoken blessings, favor, promises, and declarations over our lives.

Thank You for assuring us that Your word will not return to us void but will accomplish all that You intend and we know that Your Word will not return void. Father continue to help us to remember that You are the supplier of all of our needs and the only one that can grant promotion, favor, and increase in our lives. You bestow honor, riches, and blessings in the lives of Your children as part of the rich inheritance that is laid up for us.

Help us to be even more grateful and appreciative of blessing us with more than we can ask or think. Surely God if you take care of the birds of the air and the beasts of the field, You can provide us with abundant and overflowing blessings that our eyes have not seen, or our ears have not heard. Help us, Father, to never doubt You or Your Word. Help us not to doubt or be anxious about Your ability to supply our needs. Thank You for Your provisions that assure us that if we abide in You that we can ask for anything in the name of Jesus and He will do it. Thank You for blessing us and answering our prayers for we have confidence in Your Word and Your ability to perform it for You are faithful to do what You have spoken. We give you thanks for all of Your gifts and blessings. Amen

Meet the Needs

Protection

Oh Lord, Our God, how excellent is Your name in all the earth. We give You thanks for this is the day that You have made, and we are rejoicing for we are glad in it! We magnify Your name, and we exalt You for You are the mighty and amazing God of all creation. Thank You, Lord, for the blessings and benefits of this day in Christ and for being in the land of all of Your creation.

We ask You Father for Your divine protection and safety from all that is hurtful and harmful to us. Keep us safe from every force of darkness and evil that the enemy tries to bring upon us. We give You thanks for the strong right hand of mercy that shields us from the dangers of life and the world that we live in. We rejoice in knowing that You are always our present help and that You provide a hedge of protection around us. Thank You for all the times that You send the angelic host to accompany us to allow our safe arrival at our destinations.

Lord, we ask that You allow the precious and powerful Blood of Jesus to cover us and every mode of transportation that we travel in. Lord, we ask that Your powerful, life-giving, lifesaving, and sanctifying Word will cover us and keep us. We ask Father that as we travel to and fro to accomplish Your will as Kingdom representatives and Kingdom ambassadors in the earth, You will not allow the enemy to prey upon or attack us or our loved ones. We rejoice in knowing that You are our refuge and strong tower; You are our shield and our protector in the time of need and in the time of trouble. Continue to remind us, Lord, that You are our way of escape from the storms of life that attempt to destroy us and overpower us.

Lord if You provided a pillar of fire for the Israelites by night and a cloud by day to lead Your people out of bondage, surely You can be our shield, our protector, our way maker, our highway through every wilderness season. We are grateful Lord that in our times of distress and darkness that You keep Your strong arms of protection around us. Thank You, Lord, for protecting us from the destructive force of evil and from the plots that Satan plans for us.

Lord, we ask that no matter the strength or duration of the attacks that You will keep us covered under Your wings of protection. Your precious Blood keeps us and covers us so that the enemy's ways of evil, sin, and darkness cannot cross the bloodline and penetrate Your shield of protection. Lord You cause us to fear no evil for You are the shepherd who goes with us and goes before us. You protect us from dangers seen and unseen. Thank You Lord that You have promised to be our present help, to be with us at all times, and to never leave us nor forsake us. Therefore, we have no reason to fear. Thank You, Lord, for the security that we find in You. We ask that You will continue to bless and keep us in the name of Jesus. Amen.

Protection

Purpose

Father, we come in the name of Jesus, the name at which every knee shall bow, and every tongue confess, to say thank You for being the Lord of our lives. Hear our cries and be merciful to us for we stand in need of answered prayers. Remind us that You are our God and You have made us for Your purposes. You reign and rule so that Your will is accomplished in the earth. Lord, You have predestined us to be Your children and to partake of Your goodness and Your mercy and Your manifold blessings. You created us to do Your will in the earth. We ask that You will continue to use us for Your glory. Help us to be Your hands and feet; instruments and vessels that fulfill Your purpose for our creation.

Lord create in us a stronger desire to be intentional about fulfilling our purpose. We ask that You would help us to commit our ways to Your ways and to align our wills with Yours. Mold us and shape us as clay under the wheel of the potter so that we do only what we have been designed, created, and purposed to do. Help us to be real in all that we do and relevant in our times and seasons to make the impact needed to be Your instruments that help transform lives. Help us, Lord, to be faithful to our calling in ministry and service. Lord, we ask that You will help us to be obedient to the Spirit of the true and living God when our flesh refuses to obey Your will or pursue the mission that You have ordained. Help us, Lord, to remain focused, and Holy Spirit directed and anointed to fulfill Kingdom purpose. Help us to never forget why You created us and called us to serve and honor You. Help us to be faithful and obedient to the will, ways, and Word of God.

Lord as we throw ourselves on the altar, may our flesh be

consumed by the fires of consecration and sanctification. May our sacrifices to fulfill our purpose and obey Your will be pleasing in Your sight. Let us offer up the sacrifice of praise and obedience that is a sweet fragrance to Your nostrils. Lord help us to live our lives to the fullest, knowing that our lives and our purpose are rooted and grounded in You, our God, and our creator. Remind us that nothing is more important in life than pleasing You and serving You in all of our ways.

Let us be purpose minded and purpose directed as we submit our lives for Your glory and for Your honor. Father, we ask for Your help in letting nothing, and no one interfere with the purposes that You have ordained for our lives. Let serving You and pleasing You in all our ways be our first priority as we acknowledge You for guidance and direction. Help us to be committed to a lifestyle of purposeful living. It is unto You Lord that we give thanks for helping us to find our purpose and for giving our lives meaning and significance. Let all that You have taught us about purpose be forever seared and emblazoned in our hearts and in our minds. We ask that You would transform and conform our lives daily for Your purposes. We give You thanks for saving us and choosing us not because of our works, but according to Your own purpose and plans. Father, we are forever grateful for all that You have done and we give You thanks in the name of Jesus. Amen.

Purpose

God's Will

Father, it is in the name of Jesus, our Lord and our Savior that we humbly enter into Your presence. Thank You for the privilege to come freely and boldly before Your throne of grace. You are truly a merciful God, and we are forever grateful that You have given us the privilege and gift of prayer. We are thankful that Your will for our lives pervades in the earth. It was in Your prayer to the Father that You asked for His will to be done on earth and in heaven. Lord it is Your desire that man should forsake his evil, selfish, and fleshly ways to live a life surrendered to Your will. Let our will be surrendered and submitted to Your hands of grace and mercy.

We ask Father that You will let all that You have declared, decreed, and ordained for this world, this land, this country, this state, this city, our churches, and our lives come to pass as You have spoken. Remind us that whoever does the will of God, You call them members of Your family. Help us to be true worshippers as we strive to do Your will so that You will hear and answer our prayers and petitions.

When our flesh desires to control and lead us in the wrong direction, Lord let Your Holy Spirit rule and guide every thought and every action. Father, we ask that You would help us never to be conformed to the world or its ways and its evils, but to be transformed in our hearts and minds so that seeking Your will becomes good and acceptable for us. We ask You, Father, to let Your will dominate our thinking, our wills, our attitudes, and our behaviors. Let the ways of man take a backseat to every God ordained priority that aligns with Your Word, Your will, and Your ways.

Father, it is Your will that none should be lost or to perish, so Lord help us to make winning souls for the Kingdom to be our top priority. Help us to acknowledge You in all of our ways so that You will direct our paths according to Your will. Align our hearts and our minds with You Lord so that Your will takes pre-eminence in our lives.

Remind us, Lord, when we get caught up in ourselves that Your will abides forever; Your will is forever settled in heaven. Help us to live according to Your will and Your desires for us to live holy, upright before You and to keep Your commandments and obey Your Word.

Obedience to Your Word will help us to live fruitful and productive lives; blessed and prosperous lives. We ask for Your help Lord in sanctifying, consecrating our lives and to be holy in all our ways. Let our desire be to observe and do all that You require. We ask for Your help to live in fear and reverence of You. Then, Father, we ask in the name of Jesus that You will help us to fulfill Your will and purposes for our lives and to serve You faithfully for as long as we remain upon the earth.

It is in the mighty and matchless name of Jesus that we pray and ask these blessings. Amen.

God's Will

Healing

Father, we come in the name of Your Son Jesus, our Lord, and our Savior who died for the healing of the land and the healing of our bodies. We give You thanks for You have allowed us to know that whatever we ask in prayer, believing that we have received it, we know that it will be ours. We come in Your name, Jesus, knowing that if we cry out to You, we will be healed from all manner of sickness and disease, all manner of physical, emotional, and mental hurt. Lord, You remind us in Your Word that You are the one who heals us. You have healing powers that can cleanse us from all infirmities and impurities in our bodies, minds, souls, and spirits.

Gracious God You can even heal the brokenhearted, and You apply the balm of Gilead to comfort us in our brokenness and wounded states. Lord if You heal us, we will truly be healed. Thank You, Jesus, for carrying our sins and sickness on Your body and for hanging on the cross so that we could have more abundant lives. We ask that You remind us always of the lengths that You went to insure our healing and salvation. You were whipped and beaten beyond recognition. Precious and life-giving blood streamed from Your body because of the 39 stripes that You took for the healing of every disease. Thank You Lord for giving Your life for our healing and our well-being. You personally carried our sins and sickness in Your body so that our souls and our bodies could prosper and be in good health. Thank You, Lord, that because of Your completed work on the cross we can believe on Your word, stand on Your Word, and decree total healing for our minds and our bodies. The blood that You shed ensures deliverance from the infirmities that attempt to plague our bodies.

Father, we ask that You help us in the areas where our faith is too weak to believe for our healing. In Your name Jesus, we ask for healing over every cell, every tissue, every organ, every muscle, every nerve and every system within our bodies. Lord, we ask that You keep us in good health and that You speak to those areas of our bodies that are plagued by pain and sickness. We cry out to You Lord in our times of weakness and distress, asking You Lord to touch our bodies and speak a Word of deliverance from the ailments that torment us. Lord show us compassion and lay Your healing hands upon us, and we shall be made whole. We trust You and believe You Lord for that which we have prayed. Thank You for hearing our prayers and healing our bodies in Jesus' name. To You be all glory, and honor and praise. Amen and amen.

Healing

Warfare

Our Lord and our God, You are our Jehovah Sabaoth, our Lord of hosts, and our Lord of armies. (Names of God, Rose Publishing). We come to You in the name of Jesus for strength to do battle against the enemy and the forces of darkness. We know that the enemy comes to rob, kill, and destroy us. Lord, we are thankful that we never have to go to battle alone and that You have taught us through Your Word that our struggle is not against flesh and blood, but against powers of darkness and evil, against principalities and spiritual wickedness in high places. Continue to go before us Lord to destroy the works of the enemy. Remind us that we cannot fight a spiritual battle while in the flesh.

Help us to remember that we are to stand still and see the salvation of the Lord while You fight the battles. We ask Lord, that You will keep us strong in You and in the power of Your might. We know that Satan desires to sift us as wheat and to destroy our faith so that we will cower and fail to trust the Lord for victory. Lord, we ask that You would rescue us from every evil way and deed of the enemy. Help us to resist the devil so that he will flee from us. He comes as a roaring lion in attempts to bring fear and trepidation. Help us to remember that no weapon that he forms shall prosper against us. You have armed and equipped us with Your Word and given us the whole armor to suit up for battle with. It is with our armor that we become armed and dangerous, suited for battle against the devil and his demonic spirits.

Lord, we ask that You would fight against those who fight against us and those who try to hinder our work with all manner of evil and criticism. Let their works be destroyed by their own negativity and critical spirits. Let embarrassment come upon them and shut their mouths, except for them to pray. Cover us from ambush and attack and help us to maintain faith under fire. Let us not be guilty of friendly fire upon fellow members of the Body of Christ.

Anoint us afresh for battle so that we can be battle ready and be victorious in defeat over the forces of darkness. Send the angelic host to accompany us and let us not be war casualties of the enemy. We thank You for victory in Jesus and for the power and authority that Jesus gave through His completed work on the cross. Thank You, Lord, for making us strong and courageous in spiritual warfare so that the works of the enemy never prevail over our lives.

Having done all Lord, we will gird our loins with truth. We will put on the breastplate of righteousness; we shod our feet with the gospel of peace. Lord, we ask that You will strengthen us so that we can take up the shield of faith and the helmet of salvation. Show us how to use the sword of the Spirit so that we can cut asunder the works of the enemy through believing the strong and powerful Word of the Most High God. We thank You for being our righteous redeemer and deliverer. May we ever hold fast to the truth of Your Word so that we can remain strong against every evil word and work of the enemy. We declare victory in Your name for every battle won, for we are more than conquerors because of the finished work on the cross. We thank You and we praise You in the name of Jesus we pray. Amen

Spiritual Warfare

Mrs. Dana P. Richardson

Psalm 1:2-3 (NIV)
... but whose delight is in the law of the LORD,
and who meditates on his law day and night.
That person is like a tree planted by streams of water,
which yields its fruit in season
and whose leaf does not wither –
whatever they do prospers.

Ms. Dana Richardson is currently a Certified Lay Servant at Stewart Chapel United Methodist Church, where she serves the Lord through leading praise and worship, leads in worship, preaches, and teaches the Word of God. Dana is Chairperson of Witness Ministries, where she operates in the prophetic, encourages our congregation and community, and anyone she meets. She is a prayer warrior, a playwright, and participates in creative arts ministry. Dana has been involved in creative writing and theatrical expressions since her teens. Her ministry is biblically based, and Holy Spirit led and inspired.

Inspiration

My late parents, Rev. Dr. Samuel J. Price, Sr., and Mrs. Rebecca F. Price are the "wind beneath my wings." Their parental guidance truly is my inspiration for everything I do. Prayer is the foundation of my existence as the youngest of five children. Praise, poetry, and plays keep me grounded in my faith-walk, and I want to share some of my innermost prayers with those who need a lift or light on this journey.

Dear Jesus,

We come humbly before you, to say thank you. Thank you for all you've done for us. Simple words that express our gratitude, our time spent on bended knees to say how much we love you, and hear from you that you care. We pray. We listen. We believe that your promises are "yes" and "amen".

We have hope today.

Teach us HUMILITY to serve you and your people.

Give us OPEN minds, hands and hearts to take care of your kingdom.

PERFECT those things that concerns us, so we're not distracted by society's way of life. We know that we should be more like you, Christ like in what we say, do and how we behave.

ENCOURAGE us to sow good seeds and on good ground so in due season, we will reap the harvest if we don't faint!

As long as we remain humble, keep an open-mind, operate in God's purpose for lives, and encourage others through love, compassion and support, we experience H.O.P.E. now and always, in Jesus' name. Amen

Dear Jesus

Ever-Present Help

Lord, You are an ever-present Help in our every time of need. You are always there, shining Your light in our darkness. Even when we cannot see our way, Your unfailing Love captures our attention. It serves as a constant reminder that You are a way maker. No one can make a way like You do. No one can calm a storm like You do. No one can lift a burden like You do. No one knows Your way, but we all know that You are the Way!

I love the way You reassure us that Your plans for us are greater and never will cause us harm. We may experience pain, suffering, or even times when we feel lonely, but Your presence is everywhere. Even when we feel left out, left behind or have taken a left turn, You always extend Your hands of mercy and provide us with Grace through Your Holy Spirit that guides us into all truths.

Forgive us for those times we overlook You, and those times we went to everyone without acknowledging You first. Lord, we know that You will not fail, that You cannot leave us alone, and that You will always be our ever-present Help! Thank You, Lord for holding us close, Dear God!

Thank You for leading us to Your place of peace when our mind wanders on our different paths of life. We are so thankful that You are able to allow rest in Your Promise and provide comfort, strength, joy, and security when we need it most. In Jesus' name, we pray. Amen.

Ever-Present Help

Now unto Him

Now unto Him who is able, faithful, merciful, loving and kind. His Love is pure, His Favor lasts a lifetime, His Grace is sufficient and His faithfulness is great! He is the Great I Am! Even in the midst of a pandemic, civil unrest, troubles of this world, we have a Savior. We have an anchor in the storm. We have a safety net when it seems all hope is gone. We have a Healer of all manner of disease, a Comforter when we feel weary, worn, isolated or excluded. We have the Lifter, the Giver of Life, our All and All when we feel the pressures of an ever-changing, cold, heartless and cruel world; we have loving arms to hold us, draw us, carry us, defend us, and hide us from the enemy's traps.

We can face tomorrow knowing that He is the same yesterday, today and forever!

Now unto Him that is able to do exceeding abundantly more than we can ask, imagine or think. To the only wise God our Savior, majesty, dominion and power who is able to keep us from falling and present us faultless before His throne, our Savior Jesus the Christ.

The One who was, and is and is to come. No other can do for us like Jesus can. No other God can fix it, no other God is able, and besides Him, no other can, no other will.

We thank Him for being God all by Himself.

In Jesus' name. Amen

Now Unto Him

Calm my Fears

Lord, never in my life have I ever thought I would feel this way. Imagine me asking You such questions as "What's going on?" and "Don't You see what's happening?" or even "Where are You, Lord?" I am always wondering what next without considering that You are the same God that has rescued me before and will always be the same God to do it again. Yet, why am I scared to take the next step? Why am I afraid of what's coming next? I say that I trust You, and I believe it in my heart and mind, but my eyes are seeing it differently.

I keep repeating Psalm 23 and know that You are my Shepherd, dear Lord. I need to be comforted, and my mind needs to be at ease. My heart needs to feel Your presence, and I am waiting on You, Lord, to calm my fears. I am on my knees, with tears as my voice, dear Jesus. Please hold me near because I feel fear, I feel discomfort, and I feel pain. Lord, please help me understand that You are with me, and will never put more on me than I can bear, so I trust You and Your timing. I am asking You to once again hear my cry of help to calm my fears as I face _____(insert person, place or thing), knowing that You are always able and available to cast my anxieties away. Bring peace to my confused mind, and lift me with Your Word of hope and healing, above all that cause me any fear this day. In Jesus' name, Amen.

Calm my Fears

Like Never Before

Lord, we need you like never before. We need you to be our open door as we knock for new opportunities. While one is asking, another is receiving. While one is hoping, another is trusting. While one is thanking, another is waiting. Yet, we all are expecting to hear from you. We pray, we fast, we praise and we worship. We wait and we rejoice. We pray without ceasing, even when our faith is tested, we press on! We patiently wait our turn, despite the odds stacked against us.

Why?

Because we know you heard our cries for help, you understand our pain and anguish, you see our silent tears and feel our inner frustration because you are near to the broken-hearted; you fill us when we're empty, and cause our cups to overflow so we can be a blessing to others. As long as there is breath in our bodies, we will always have a reason to pray, say thank you, ask forgiveness and have the courage to see how You will bless our hands, our hearts that gives us hope!

Thank you for providing us with hope, healing and happiness. Amen

Like Never Before

This One's Personal!

Dear Lord, oh Jesus, You are my everything. You have proven Your love for me over and over again. You have shown me favor, You have given me more than I've ever hoped for, asked, or imagined.

Now, I need You, Lord, to meet a special need, to lend Your ear to an immediate request, and to answer swiftly as I call on Your powerful name. This time it's personal! Not for selfish gain, or impure motives, my God, I just need You to hear me. I need You to help me, and I need You to heal me because You said to ask, and it will be given, so I am standing, praying, fasting, expecting and trusting that You will be an on-time God!

Please Lord, God, I call forth a personal touch, a personal embrace and a personal release of Your Power because I'm grateful for Your steadfast Love shown toward me and I'm in need of Your constant care. Lord, please don't delay because I need You now, right now, and it's personal! In Jesus' name, Amen.

This one's Personal

Dearly Beloved, We Gather Together

Lord, as I reflect on the start of wedding vows that so many couples have made and promised, Father God, I can't help but reflect on our first vow to You. I know we've made a vow to keep believing and serving You, Lord. Lord, teach us how to live and love as the first day we recited our vows to each other, as we have also made this commitment to You, dear God.

Remind us of our roles that we play and the patience, understanding, and wisdom that only You can give couples to have and to hold. Having little or having plenty means we work together to share our blessings with each other and bless those around us that we hold dear to our hearts. In sickness, let us be sensitive to the needs of our spouses, and in health, let us never grow weary in doing good physically, mentally, emotionally, socially, financially and more importantly, spiritually. Lord, let us always make time to be an Ecclesiastes 3 couple when choosing how and when we spend time together.

Time is something we cannot get back, so always lead us and guide us Lord through our decisions. Let us take each step by step to love and to cherish. Dear Lord, help us to bring You our plans so we may succeed, knowing everything operates in Your perfect timing and order. Help us, Father God, to build a strong foundation of trust and honesty, sharing our weaknesses and secrets, and relying on each other's' strengths. As we gather together, Lord, let us recognize that we are ministering as life partners, knowing our steps are ordered, our days are numbered, and our blessings are ordained by God.

Forgive us when we speak out of turn, step ahead of Your plans without acknowledging You first, or even times You need

121

us to step aside, dear Jesus. Lord, I thank You for my marriage, my spouse, and my home. Fill our hearts, with love, igniting the passion we've had since date one. Keep us prayerful, cheerful, and thankful for each other, in the vows we forever live, until we are separated by death. In Jesus' name, Amen.

Dearly Beloved

Breath Prayer

Lord, I come to You, not asking for anything. I come to You with thanksgiving for the air I breathe. As I breathe in, I take in the wonderful blessing of life. I realize that You are my Life! As I breathe out, I exhale that You are my Sustainer. I am able to live out the desires of my heart because You are my Keeper.

Dear Jesus, I just want to say thank You for every breath that You give. In Jesus' name, Amen

Breath Prayer

_____
_____
_____
_____
_____
_____
_____
_____
_____
_____
_____
_____
_____
_____
_____
_____
_____
_____
_____

Help My Unbelief!

Father God, in the name of Jesus, I ask You right now to make me a believer again. I've witnessed what You've done in my life before and can't help but tell thank You for all You've done. Help me to see Your vision when my eyes are blurred. Help me to know that You have a far and better plan for my life. Right now, there are clouds of doubt and waves of disappointments that are bringing feelings of despair and disbelief.

I don't want to waver in my faith, so I am coming to You, Lord Jesus, asking humbly that You help my unbelief! Father, God, change my way of thinking and let me think on things that are pure and noteworthy. Lord, I have seen Your works, and I've witnessed what You've done for others. I know that You are able to do anything for anyone, so I need You to do this for me! I am sorry for feeling the way I do, but yet You know I'm human.

I know You love me and care so much for me, so please make me a believer of Your Word again. I ask that You show me Your marvelous works one more time, so I can believe again. In Jesus' name, Amen.

Help my Unbelief

When Joy Comes

Father of Peace and Comfort, we know You give us Your Daily Bread. Your Word is our guiding light and provides life to us today. Your Word is our hope and helps us expect greater things to come tomorrow. We know Your Word will always stand. I am asking You, Dear God, to wipe tears of those in sadness and sorrow. I am asking You, Father, to strengthen the weak and the weary. God, I come to You, calling on and trusting Your Son, Jesus, who promised us a Comforter, The Holy Spirit, in our darkest hour and in our dry Season.

Someone's mourning, someone's lonely, and someone's in need of Your presence in their lives today, so please bring joy to their spirit, bring comfort to their soul and bring peace to their mind. We are thankful for Your presence in the midst of our storms, so please let us feel Joy again. We will be so grateful when Joy comes. In Jesus' name, Amen.

When Joy Comes

While Others Are Calling

Lord, I can call on Your name, Jesus, and know that I get Your attention. Whether morning, noon or night, I can trust that You will meet all of my needs. So many needs and so many names, yet while others are calling, You hear my voice. You know me well. You rescue me. You provide for me. For that, I just want to say thank You and know that while others are calling, bless them too, for You are a God who knows it all and provides for all of Your children.

Remember my prayer, dear Jesus, while others are calling on Your name, please don't forget about me. In Jesus' name, Amen.

While Others Are Calling

_____
_____
_____
_____
_____
_____
_____
_____
_____
_____
_____
_____
_____
_____
_____
_____
_____
_____

Lord, Lift Me!

Lord, it has been one thing after another. Yet, I'm reminded that trouble we will have in this world always. I'm thankful that trouble doesn't last always. I choose to respond to trouble by coming to You in prayer. Lord, only You are able to lift me above what my eyes can see. I am looking to You, as my Helper and my Guide. Only You, dear God, can lift me beyond the circumstances that are in my path.

Dear Lord, only You can lift me to a place higher than I. I am so glad that You can see past my hurts, and understand my body language while in pain. I know by faith, You are working behind the scenes, and Your hands are moving mightily, working all things out for me. I can feel Your hand lifting me close, guiding me further down the journey and reaching out to see about me. I thank You, Lord, for always being there to lift me up when otherwise I would fall down. In Jesus' name, Amen.

Lord Lift Me

_____
_____
_____
_____
_____
_____
_____
_____
_____
_____
_____
_____

Lord, Prepare Me

Lord, prepare me for what's to come, even though I may find it hard to handle or difficult to understand. Help me to ask for wisdom and guide me with Your Hand. For if You are preparing it for me, then there is a better plan bigger than what I can see right now. I know You've paced the best care into the works of whatever it is that You're preparing me for.

Lord, Jesus, please prepare me even though I'm afraid, I know You'll never leave me alone. You promised to keep watch over me, and that is in everything I do and say that brings You Glory.

I am asking You to keep a hedge of protection around me. Remind me that You have commanded angels to have charge over my life. Lord, prepare me for whatever comes what may and accept what You allow in my life. For I know my life is in Your hands. Lord, prepare my heart, my mind, my soul, and my spirit for whatever it is, for I know that You know what's best and have already prepared it. In Jesus' name, Amen.

Lord Prepare Me

Mrs. Sherri Pinckney Kinloch
Philippians 4:10-13

I rejoiced in the Lord greatly that now at length you have revived your concern for me. You were indeed concerned for me, but you had no opportunity. Not that I am speaking of being in need, for I have learned in whatever situation I am to be content. I know how to be brought low, and I know how to abound. In any and every circumstance, I have learned the secret of facing plenty and hunger, abundance and need. I can do all things through him who strengthens me.

Mrs. Sherri Pinckney Kinloch. I, like many others, have endured many hardships in life, but during one of the darkest hours of my life, God spoke to me through a verse of scripture found in Joel 2:25-26 that says, "...I will restore to you the years that the locust hath eaten, the cankerworm, and the caterpillar, and the palmerworm, my great army which I sent among you. And ye shall eat in plenty, and be satisfied, and praise the name of the Lord your God that hath dealt wondrously with you: and my people shall never be ashamed." God promised me greater for all of the suffering that I endured, and He promised me that I would never experience the shame of my past ever again. During my downward spiral, I still had enough faith in God's unwavering love for me. I came into this world with a purpose, and as long I continue to trust and obey His instructions, He'll provide what is needed to take me to the promises that He has for me.

The odds were stacked against me, but God's favor, grace and mercy kept me from losing my mind, from falling into depression, from taking drugs or abusing alcohol to numb the hurt and the pain that I felt. I was sexually assaulted and bullied as a very young child; raped as a teenager on my very first date and suffered through an emotionally abusive relationship in my teens that resulted in pregnancy. At that time in my life, I felt like unloved and undeserving of love, but what the enemy thought would destroy, God allowed it to bless me. God used this unplanned pregnancy to show me that I could do something good. I was capable of loving someone and more importantly, He gave me someone that always showed me love. I never expected to be a teen mother or a mother at all for that matter, but I received one of the greatest gifts when I was blessed to become Rashad's Mom. He completely changed my life!!

That lack of self-love led me to engage in very unhealthy relationships where I suffered years of physical and emotional abuse at the hands of men who claimed to love me. I didn't know it then, and I didn't understand why God would allow me to experience so much pain. Was I a horrible person and God was punishing me, or did He just forget about me? Neither of these things were true, but the enemy knew exactly what he was doing. The enemy came to destroy me, but God had a purpose for my pain. He spoke to my heart and let me know that every tear that I shed, and every sleepless night, and every struggle that I endured, was necessary for Him to make me into the strong woman of God that I am today.

In the midst of my struggles, God allowed me (after eight years of going to school at night, while working a full-time and part-time job, and being a single mother) to be the first person, in my immediate family, to graduate from college. Through the encouragement, love, and support of my parents, I was able to obtain a Bachelor of Science in Business Management degree at the age of 35 and I have been blessed to have a great career in Property and Project Management for the past 20 years. He has also blessed me to finally have the love that I always wanted and needed with my husband, Derrick and two bonus children; Derrick Jr. and Essence. I now have my beautiful blended family! My life is a living testimony of God's grace, His favor and His love! Someone is going through a difficult time, and they've lost faith in themselves, lost faith in their family, and lost faith in God's love for them. He is using me as a vessel to pour into you what He has poured into to me, to give you hope for tomorrow. A brighter day is coming! You may be weeping right now, but joy is on the way! (Psalms 30:5)

Inspiration

God made me a promise in 2014, and all I had to do in order to get to this promise was to trust Him, have faith in Him and His plan for me, and be obedient. I did, and He has given me double for my troubles! He restored everything that I lost and has given me more than I ever had. He gave me a love that I have never had, and He has allowed me to make peace with my past. So, I can say this with joy and confidence. I know that my God is faithful and just and He is using me for His glory, so I'm "...forgetting those things which are behind and reaching forth unto those things which are before. I press toward the mark for the prize of the high calling of God in Christ Jesus" (Philippians 3:13-14), and because I know who I am in Him I give Him all praises for the good, the bad and the ugly because He worked it out for my good!!

The prayers that I've written came through quiet meditation and reflection on the goodness of God in my life, and all that He has brought me through. Nothing can separate me from His love!! I know that now!

May God bless you as you read these prayers and may the words that you read inspire you, captivate you, comfort you, and bless your soul.

God bless!

136

Strength

Mighty God, in whom I look to for strength and protection. Blessing, glory, and honor all belong to You.

I ask that as I begin my journey today in this thing called life, that You shield, cover, and protect me from the hands of the enemy.

I ask that You would allow Your angels to surround me, and protect me from seen and unseen dangers, plots, schemes, and plans that the enemy has devised for my destruction.

I ask that You show up in this situation and cause my enemies to fall at my feet, cause those things that were meant to destroy me to bless me, cause those things that were meant to defeat me to be defeated.

I know that as Your child, that if I ask anything in Your name, it shall be done, so I declare that victory is mine. I declare that no weapon formed against me shall prosper, and I declare that this prayer will be heard and answered in the name of Jesus! Amen.

A faithful God does not expect you to do what you cannot;

He supplies the needed strength.

ERWIN W. LUTZER

Strength

How did you depend on God for spiritual, emotional, or physical strength today?

Gratefulness

Compassionate God, I come to You today with a grateful heart full of praise for You and how You constantly and consistently shower me with Your love.

Even when I fall short in doing or saying the things I should, You are still faithful to me.

Thank You for never giving up on me, and for gently leading me with Your love, and tender guidance.

Allow Your light to shine in and through my life, so that others may be able to see it and desire to know the God that I love and serve for themselves.

Let there be a word, deed, or action that comes forth from being that will be a blessing to someone today.

I declare this to be done in the name of Jesus! Amen.

Gratefulness

Today, I am grateful to God for...

Healing

Oh, Father God, I thank You for allowing me to see another day. I'm thankful to You, God, because the doctor's report was not the final report. I thank You, oh God, for touching me with Your finger of love, for healing my body, dear Father, again and again. I thank You for removing the sickness and disease from my body. I thank You for total and complete healing in the name of Jesus.

I ask, dear God, that You pour out Your blood so that it cleanses me of all unrighteousness, and all iniquity. Make me whole just as You did with the woman with the issue of blood. I know that a touch from You will bring forth healing dear God, so I thank You for my healing.

I thank You for how You've prepared the physicians and the nurses and everyone that will participate in my healing and care through this process. I thank You, God, for how You're going to use them, Holy Father to bless me. I declare and decree this to be so in Jesus' name, Amen!!

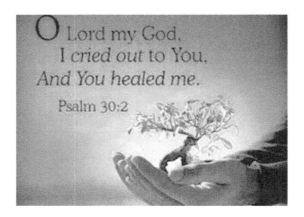

O Lord my God,
I cried out to You,
And You healed me.

Psalm 30:2

Healing

God I ask that you look into my heart today and heal...

Mercy

Merciful God, full of compassion, love, and grace, I'm thankful for how You have allowed me to see another glorious day that You have created. The sunlight shown on my face, I awakened refreshed and renewed and I slept peacefully through the night in a comfortable bed. I know that it is only because of Your love that I had a place to lay my head, food to eat, and shelter from the dangers of this world. I can't give You enough praise for all of the many things that You do for me, my family, and loved ones.

I never want to forget those that are less fortunate than I am. I know that You see them and know them all by name, so I ask dear God for an extra portion of love, compassion, grace, and deliverance upon my brother or my sister that for reasons that are unknown to me, have found themselves in situations that they can't find their way out of.

Touch their hearts, my Master, draw them nearer, so that they will come running towards You and they can begin life anew. Speak to their hearts so that a word, deed, or action would touch them in a special way and in that moment they would feel Your presence.

I thank You for the souls that will be delivered, and the blessings that will come from faith and obedience to Your Word. I thank You, I praise You, and I exalt You! In the name of Jesus, Amen.

Mercy

God, You showed me so much mercy when you...

Marriage

Holy Father, we know that there is power in unity. The enemy knows that if he can divide us, he can destroy us. When a man and woman come together as one in Holy Matrimony, the power that they possess is multiplied. You are not a threat to the enemy when You indulge in premarital sex or others actions that God ordained for a man and his wife, but when You decide to become one, it destroys the enemies plan for Your destruction.

My prayer, oh God, is that You would allow this marriage bond to be built on a foundation of love for You, love, honor, respect and loyalty to each other and to be overflowing with compassion and understanding. We commit ourselves totally and completely to You, so that You may be glorified through this marriage. Let others see this union and desire to have the same relationship or better with their spouses.

We know that there will be disagreements, but let those disagreements be resolved peacefully and respectfully. You said in Your Word that *a man that findeth a wife finds a good thing*; so, let that same joy that he felt when he found her continue to shower blessings upon their union. We declare and decree a marriage filled with love and longevity. In the name of Jesus, Amen.

Marriage Takes Three to be complete,
it's not enough for two people to meet.
They must be united in love by love's creator, God Above.
A marriage that follows God's plan takes more than a woman
and a man. It needs oneness that can be only from Christ.
Marriage Takes Three.

Marriage

God I ask that You bless my marriage today, so that…

_____

_____

_____

_____

_____

_____

_____

_____

_____

_____

_____

_____

_____

_____

_____

_____

_____

_____

_____

_____

Be Steadfast

Dear Lord, when my enemies and those that say that they love me, allow Satan to use them, help me to lean on Your Word and be reminded that You are "...not deceived;... for whatsoever a man soweth that shall he also reap. For he that soweth to his flesh shall of the flesh reap corruption, but he that soweth to the Spirit shall of the Spirit reap life everlasting." Strengthen me so that I will ".... not be weary in well-doing", and trust You and know that Your promises are true and that if I hold on and wait on you, in due season, I will reap if I faint not." (Gal 6:7-9).

In other words, my breakthrough is on the way. My deliverance is on the way. I'm about to walk into the purpose and the promise that You prepared just for me. So, keep me humbled God.

Let me be steadfast, immovable and always abounding in the work of the Lord. (I Corinthians 15:58) Don't let my labor be in vain, don't let my suffering and my heartache be in vain, don't let my enemies rejoice over me. In the name of Jesus, I pray, Amen.

Steadfast

I will continue to be steadfast today, because God is leading me to do…

_____
_____
_____
_____
_____
_____
_____
_____
_____
_____
_____
_____
_____
_____
_____
_____
_____
_____
_____
_____
_____
_____
_____
_____
_____
_____
_____
_____
_____
_____

Hope

Blessings, glory, and honor all belong to You and only You, oh Lord. You are my help, my strength, and my redeemer. It's in the lowest places in my life that I find safety in Your arms. You are my rock, my deliverer and my peace. When I had given up on myself and couldn't see a brighter day ahead, You reminded me that I am fearfully and wonderfully made. You reminded me that because I am Your child, there isn't anything good that You will withhold from me.

You reminded me that I shouldn't grow weary in well-doing, because if I keep on believing, keep on trusting, and hold on just a little while longer, I would have wings like an eagle and be able to soar above the negativity, heartbreak, depression, and anxiety in my life.

You give me hope for tomorrow, and each day that I have life, I'm going to praise You, honor You, and magnify Your Holy and righteous name. Thank You for Your love. In the name of Jesus, I pray, Amen.

Hope

God, my hope for today is...

Honor

Almighty God, my deliverer, and my protector, "Have mercy upon me, oh God, according to Your loving-kindness, according to the multitude of Your tender mercies, blot out my transgressions, wash me thoroughly from my iniquity and cleanse me from my sin." (Psalms 51:1-2).

Heavenly Father, when I call on You, You answer. When I need You, You are always there. You are sovereign, merciful, and worthy of all of my praise. There is not a need that You haven't met, there is not a problem that You haven't solved, and there's no one in my life that loves me like You do. You've seen me at my best and at my worse, and You never turned away from me.

You kept on loving me through my periods of disobedience. You loved me when I fell short and waited for me to return to You, and I'm so grateful for the opportunity to say I'm Your child and You are my Heavenly Father. I will bless Your name, forevermore. In Jesus' name, Amen.

Honor

God I will honor you today by...

Glory

"Bless the Lord, O my soul: and all that is within me, bless his Holy name." (Psalm 103:1) God of Heaven and of Earth. My Alpha and my Omega. My help in troubling times. You've allowed the plans of my enemies to fail. You've allowed me to prosper in the midst of turmoil in my life, You've caused my enemy's wicked plans to work for my good, and You've caused my enemies to bless me and left them confused.

When I reflect on just how good, how GREAT, and how awesome You are, I can't stop giving You glory, honor, and praise. I will forever bless Your name. Thank You for life, health and strength. Thank You for blessing me beyond measure. Thank You for answered and unanswered prayers.

Thank You for smoothing out the rough edges of my life and making my crooked paths straight. Thank You for just being God Almighty! In the name of Jesus, I pray, Amen.

Glory

God allow Your glory to be revealed in my life today as I…

Praise

"Great is Thy faithfulness," O God my Father, There is no shadow of turning with Thee; Thou changest not, Thy compassions, they fail not As Thou hast been Thou forever wilt be." (Song by Chris Rice, written By Thomas O. Chisolm.) Your love never waivers, Your love never fails.

Your love for me awakens my spirit daily and causes my soul to desire more of You. To know more, to fellowship with You more, to love You more.

My heart leaps for joy at the very mention of Your name. My excitement can't be contained when I think of where You've brought me from, and what You've brought me out of.

I can't help but lift my voice and shout hallelujah to the Most High God. You promised in Your word that "When thou passest through the waters, I will be with thee; and through the rivers, they shall not overflow thee: when thou walkest through the fire, thou shalt not be burned; neither shall the flame kindle upon thee." (Isaiah 43:2)

I will continue to lift up Your name, to exalt You, and worship You my God. Nothing I have exists without You, nothing I do is without You, and I will reverence You all the days of my life. In the name of Jesus, Amen.

Praise

No matter what happens in my life today, I praise God because He has...

_____

_____

_____

_____

_____

_____

_____

_____

_____

_____

_____

_____

_____

_____

_____

_____

_____

_____

_____

_____

_____

_____

_____

_____

_____

_____

_____

_____

_____

_____

_____

Purpose

Heavenly Father, I know that we all came into this world with a predestined purpose. I know that Your plans for my life are great and that You have already placed the right people in my life, given me enough faith, and blessed me with enough favor to accomplish it all.

I come seeking your guidance, Your protection, and Your grace. Help me to stay strong in my faith and focus on the things that will honor You. You are the center of my joy and You are the reason for my peace.

Help me, oh Lord, to run the race that you set before me with determination, faith and endurance.

Help me, oh Lord, so that when things don't look the way I want them to look, or the outcome doesn't meet my expectations, to know that I need to trust Your plan for my life.

You are the Author and Finisher of my faith. Your timing is impeccable, and Your grace is sufficient! I honor You today God with my lips, life, and my love. In Jesus' name, AMEN

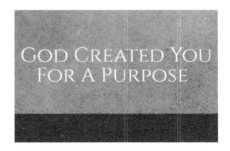

Purpose

God, I know Your purpose for giving me life is to…

PURPOSE
God's purpose for your life was determined before you were in your Mother's womb

PREPARATION
To fulfill God's purpose for your life, you must prepare for the journey by praying, and asking God for guidance

PROVISIONS
Don't look at the situation and talk yourself out of pressing forward. You are inadequate when you seek to do things on your own, but with God you can do it all. If God brought you to it, He will bring you through it.

PROMISE
Once you have embraced your purpose, prepared for the journey, and God has provided you with all that you need, you can confidently walk into the Promised Land that God has created especially for you!

Trust God's vision and His plan for your life!

AMEN

Author
Sherri Pinckney Kinloch

Quotes: The Power of God through the Power of Prayer

The power of God is the very essence of the life of God Himself. It is the supernatural energy that radiates from God's being. This supernatural and divine energy or power fills and indwells the bodies and souls of every born-again believer.

Prayer is important because it's an opportunity to spend intimate time with God. To truly understand the heart of God, you need to pray. John 15:15, Jesus says, "He no longer calls us His servants, but calls us His friends". Talking with God cultivates a deeper relationship with Him through adoration, repentance, thanksgiving and supplication.

Prayer strengthens the heart of a believer through the power of the Spirit. Unwavering prayers also releases the power of God's blessing on your life and in your circumstances. Jesus said, "When you pray, go into your room, close the door and pray to your Father, who is unseen."

When we decide to truly live for Christ, we pray according to His will and not our own. Through the power of prayer, we can experience God and grow our faith in Him. Whenever you feel discouraged, remember that God works through our lives when we give our heart to Him.

Prayer establishes us to the Great Companion who meets our human mind with His divine response. When you have learned to pray, you are no longer alone in the universe. You are living in the Father's house.

When you spend quality time with God in prayer, He keeps you with His power, with His boldness and give you utterance to speak His Word. Then He will stretch out His hand confirming His Word with signs and wonders.

Prayer is raising your heart to God or requesting good things from God.

In prayer, it is better to have a heart without words than words without heart.

A.M.E.N.

Agree with God
Move with God
End with God
Never Doubt God

Made in the USA
Coppell, TX
11 September 2021